HIGH COMMANDERS OF
THE ROYAL AIR FORCE

MINISTRY OF DEFENCE
AIR HISTORICAL BRANCH (RAF)

High Commanders of the Royal Air Force

Air Commodore Henry Probert

LONDON: HMSO

ISBN 0 11 772635 4

THE AIR HISTORICAL BRANCH (RAF)

The Air Historical Branch is located within the Air Force Department of the Ministry of Defence. Its tasks include preserving the historical archive of the Royal Air Force, answering historical enquiries, and research and writing. This volume is one of several AHB histories to be placed on public sale. The author has been given full access to official documents. He alone is responsible for the statements made and the views expressed.

HMSO publications are available from:

HMSO Publications Centre
(Mail and telephone orders only)
PO Box 276, London, SW8 5DT
Telephone orders 071-873-9090
General enquiries 071-873 0011
(queuing system in operation for both numbers)

HMSO Bookshops
49 High Holborn, London, WC1V 6HB   071-873 0011 (counter service only)
258 Broad Street, Birmingham, B1 2HE   021-643 3740
Southey House, 33 Wine Street, Bristol, BS1 2BQ   (0272) 264306
9-21 Princess Street, Manchester, M60 8AS   061-834 7201
80 Chichester Street, Belfast, BT1 4JY   (0232) 238451
71 Lothian Road, Edinburgh, EH3 9AZ   031-228 4181

HMSO's Accredited Agents
(see Yellow Pages)

and through good booksellers

Printed in the United Kingdom for HMSO
Dd 290189 C30 02/91

Contents

Illustrations

Foreword: By The Right Honourable The Lord Shackleton KG

Shortly after I was elected to Parliament (January 1946) and still in RAF uniform, I was sent for by "Boom" Trenchard. Conscious of the tremendous importance of this great man as father of the Royal Air Force, I duly presented myself and was smartly given a couple of Martinis. After a few moments, Lord Trenchard said "I have something serious to say to you". I clicked my heels and said "Yes, sir". He spoke "I expect you to support your party on all occasions in Parliament, except where the RAF is concerned. On those occasions you will support the RAF". I can honestly say that I always did and so did the rest of us.

Indeed at the time of the attempted take-over of Coastal Command (in which I had myself served) all RAF MPs, irrespective of party, banded together to resist Lord Mountbatten's initiative. We had (I may say quite improperly) the full co-operation not only of the Secretary of State for Air, Geordie Ward, but also of the staff. Indeed, I remember being briefed specially by Teddy Hudleston, Vice-Chief of Air Staff. The attack I am happy to say was repulsed. The independence of the RAF, as one of the three fighting services, is a continuing theme of this study by Air Commodore Probert of all former Chiefs of the Air Staff, and of three other highly distinguished commanders from World War II.

It certainly is a widely held view that the Battle of Britian could not have been won except by a unified Service, but this story of the Chiefs of the Air Staff records much more than just a struggle for independence. The significance of air power itself comes out broadly in the lives of the men who held the top post in the RAF.

Henry Probert does not try to single out any particular Chief of the Air Staff for special study and merit, but it is clear that they were all distinctive individuals of high ability and dedication who enabled the potential of air power both in peacetime operations and in war to be properly realised. What is more, as members of the Chiefs of Staff Committee they played a very full part in the evolution of British strategy over more than 70 years.

It will be a complaint against this book that the section on each Chief of the Air Staff touches on issues and interesting events which one would like to see more fully developed. But gradually a pattern emerges. What also emerges is the integrity of the men themselves, almost all of whom had fought and miraculously survived in air operations in two world wars. Not unimportant too is the intellectual quality of all, which is particularly striking in certain individuals, but Henry Probert makes no attempt other than to treat each individual with fairness and sympathy.

This book in an unusual and interesting format contrives, in fact, to reflect the whole story of the Royal Air Force.

Acknowledgements

First and foremost I wish to acknowledge the advice and assistance I have received either from individual officers whose careers are featured in this book or from their next of kin: the late Lord Trenchard, Mr Bonar Sykes, Lord Newall, Lord Dowding, Lady Portal, Mr Anthony Harris, Lady Douglas, Lord Tedder, Group Captain John Slessor, Lady Dickson, Sir Dermot Boyle, Lady Pike, Lord Elworthy, Sir John Grandy, Sir Denis Spotswood, Lady Humphrey, Lady Cameron, Sir Michael Beetham, Sir Keith Williamson, and Sir David Craig. All have been most helpful and understanding, and several have also provided photographs from their private collections.

Sir Michael Beetham has given further support in his capacity as Chairman of the Trustees of the RAF Museum, and it is thanks to him that Lord Shackleton kindly agreed to write the Foreword. The RAF Museum has, of course, been associated with this project throughout, and my thanks go to Dr John Tanner and Dr Michael Fopp, successive Directors, to Mr Chris Elliott, Keeper of Photographs, and Group Captain Bill Randle, who as the Appeals Director was the initiator of the whole scheme.

I have greatly appreciated, too, the comments and suggestions of several friends who read some of the earlier biographies in draft, notably Air Chief Marshals Sir Christopher Foxley-Norris and Sir Michael Armitage, and Mr Cecil James, and I thank particularly my professional colleagues in the Air Historical Branch – Group Captains Ian Madelin, Terry Flanagan and Geoff Thorburn, and Mr Seb Cox – who have perused all the drafts and proffered many most helpful ideas.

I am most grateful, also, to all who have helped on the production side: the typing staffs, notably Mrs Shirley Creed, the publishing staffs at HMSO under my friend Keith Riley, and the photographic staff in MOD Reprographic Services. Finally my thanks go to Denis Bateman, who assisted my research on the earlier biographies, and to his successor Squadron Leader Peter Singleton, who has not only helped obtain most of the photographs but lent an ever willing hand in many other ways, not least in compiling the index.

Introduction

Some four years ago I was invited on behalf of the Royal Air Force Museum to write short biographies of all our Chiefs of the Air Staff and of three other very senior RAF commanders. These accounts were to be published in support of a series of commemorative covers which were being issued in order to raise funds for the Museum. I accepted the invitation only after much thought. While a great deal had already been written about some of our high commanders, especially Lord Trenchard and those who had led the RAF during the Second World War, many were relatively unknown and their careers would require close research. Moreover I should have to take careful account of family and personal views and sensitivities.

At the same time the RAF Museum was a cause I was very keen to support, and it was agreed the RAF Benevolent Fund would also benefit from my work. In addition I felt that here was an opportunity to make what I hoped would come to be regarded as a worthwhile contribution to the history of the RAF. There is a plethora of books about our many different types of aircraft, about the various campaigns and operations in which the RAF has been engaged in the 70 years of its history, and about its heroes, but little has been written about most of those who have held the highest appointment the Service has to offer.

Of the 22 officers featured here, 19 were Chiefs of the Air Staff and thus (apart from Sir Frederick Sykes) reached the rank of Marshal of the Royal Air Force. That rank has, with but two exceptions, always been reserved for the CAS, and has usually been attained only towards or at the end of his tour of duty. These exceptions were Lord Douglas and Sir Arthur Harris, both of whom were promoted to MRAF at the end of World War II, and it has seemed right to include them in this volume. There remains one other distinction whose possession also justifies inclusion. Over the 70 years of its history only eight of the RAF's high commanders have been created Peers of the Realm, six of whom have been Chiefs of the Air Staff and the seventh of them Douglas. It is surely proper, therefore, to include the eighth, even though he was never promoted to the highest rank the Service can bestow. So Lord Dowding completes the tally.

My sources have varied widely; for many of the earlier figures I have been able to draw on biographies, autobiographies and memoirs, together with general histories of the period, the more important of which are listed in the bibliography. The Dictionary of National Biography has also been useful, alongside obituaries and other items which are filed away in the Air Historical Branch, including summaries of records of service. For those who are still alive most such sources do not apply, but instead I have had the inestimable advantage of being able to talk directly to them. Altogether I have met personally at some time or other 12 of the 22 officers I have written about, and for most of them I have been able to draw on the texts of lengthy confidential interviews.

I must stress at this point that the individuals featured, or their next-of-kin, were all officially approached before the project was started; as a result in all but two cases I have been able to submit my drafts to those most closely concerned. Their comments and suggestions have enabled me to correct inaccuracies and at times incorporate further points, and I wish to acknowledge all the help and encouragement I have received. Some, of course, wished I could have written at greater length, but I have felt it right to try to preserve a balance, and while some of the biographies are a little shorter none exceeds 2500 words.

Partly because of this, but primarily in order to avoid tedious repetition, I have only occasionally mentioned ranks and promotions; most of the careers I describe followed a standard progression which will be familiar to the informed reader. In the Appendix, however, each officer's record of service is summarised, and here too are details of his Service honours and awards, which I have omitted from the main text except on a few occasions where the citations have seemed specially significant. I have also excluded all reference to family circumstances, again mainly on grounds of length, but must observe here that our Chiefs – apart from Sir Edward Ellington, who was single – have invariably been fully supported by their wives; indeed in many cases that support has been a major factor in their success.

A further limitation, but inevitable under the circumstances under which I have been writing, is the absence of comparisons and, in many cases, of evaluation. Given that there have now been 19 Chiefs of the Air Staff, each bringing to some extent different qualities to the job, it stands to reason that some must have been better at it than others, but to make any kind of valid judgement one would first have to establish a whole range of criteria, and if one thing is certain it is that at least some of these criteria would depend on the circumstances of the day. To take just one very obvious example, could one really compare Trenchard with Portal? Not only were they very different types of men but one had to cope with fighting for and building an air force while the other had to lead that air force in war. As I was several times reminded during my interviews, every Chief faces a different set of circumstances, different challenges, and one must be careful of alleging that one did better than another. This is not to say that such comparisons are impossible to make. To have any validity, however, they would need to be based on far deeper research than I have been able to undertake, and in any case one needs the perspective that only time can bring; it would be impossible – indeed improper – to attempt a relative judgement at this stage on the Chiefs of the last thirty years.

Evaluation of individual contributions is a somewhat different matter, and with the earlier commanders I have usually attempted an appraisal. Here I have had the advantage of being able to draw on and compare the views of contemporaries and historians, and I hope my conclusions will be thought fair. Some readers may think me too kind, and certainly I have tried to stress the positive achievements of my subjects, giving credit where it is due. I think it needs to be remembered that all had reached highly important, responsible positions and could be expected to make a good job of them. With the later commanders, especially those who are still alive, I have kept my accounts totally factual; here the appraisals must await later historians, but maybe the detail contained here, coupled eventually with the full text of my interviews, will assist the process.

Some general observations can, however, be made. The first is obvious: no standard pattern underlies the careers of the RAF's 19 Chiefs. The first nine had all served in the First World War, all but one (Sir William Dickson) in the Royal Flying Corps, having learnt to fly either before or during that war. All, therefore, were founder members of the Royal Air Force. Of the remaining ten, eight joined the RAF before or during World War II and only the last two entered afterwards. Of these ten, four followed the route hoped for by Trenchard, joining as Flight Cadets at Cranwell, and four more came in as direct entrants, one of them as a Sergeant Pilot in the RAFVR. Perhaps surprisingly in an era when so much premium is laid on the importance of university education, only two of the ten were graduates. Their RAF careers, too, differed widely – in part reflecting the changing nature and tasks of the Service – and all one can really say is that the absence of a set pattern reflects the fact that the RAF is a young Service which has had to draw into the ranks of its officers a very wide cross-section of the nation's talent. Indeed it is not just from our own country that the RAF's leaders have come, for two of its Chiefs were born in Southern Ireland and one in New Zealand.

A second observation is that luck has inevitably played its part. There has been the luck of survival in war, when many of one's contemporaries have lost their lives. Flying is a dangerous business – in peace as well as in war. Luck has also come into it in terms of the right posting at the right time. While it is true, particularly in more recent years, that much effort goes into trying to spot the most promising officers early on and to ensure they are given the right kind of career, the element of chance is always present, and all Chiefs will readily admit to having received a spot of good fortune along the way. Nor should we forget that on two occasions chance has been the final deciding factor. Edward Ellington would never have been appointed CAS but for the sudden death of Geoffrey Salmond, and Neil Cameron became CDS only because of the death of Andrew Humphrey.

This prompts a third observation. At times it has certainly appeared to the RAF at large that one particular man was bound to be the next CAS, and often – but not always – we have been right. At other times it has been far from obvious. Often, therefore, there have been other very senior officers whose claims to the highest office have appeared equally strong and who would probably have done the job just as well had they been chosen. Moreover, having been passed by, they have often had to continue in the Service, working alongside the man who has been preferred. The selection of Cyril Newall in 1937 is a case in point, for both Hugh Dowding and Edgar Ludlow-Hewitt believed they were in with a good chance, and both continued to hold highly important posts throughout Newall's term of office. Again, when Charles Portal was appointed in late 1940, it was in preference to the highly experienced and well thought of Wilfrid Freeman, who remained Portal's right-hand man for much of the war. It would not be proper for me to comment here on other 'near-misses' of more recent years, but readers of these biographies will I hope bear in mind that for every CAS there were at least two or three contemporaries who might very easily have had the job instead.

This leads to a fourth general point, namely that all Chiefs have depended on the loyal support and assistance of their senior Service colleagues, and they will be the first to admit that their achievements have been largely those of the team they have led; indeed most Chiefs have previously served in one of the Principal Staff Officer posts on the Air Council or the Air Force Board and therefore have known how the system worked. It is not, however, just the Service officers that one must remember. Until very recently there were also the Secretaries to the Air Ministry, the Permanent Under-Secretaries or, in later years, the Deputy Under-Secretaries. These were very senior civil servants, usually long experienced in the ways of the Air Ministry or Air Force Department and of the Whitehall machine, and no CAS could have survived without establishing a close rapport with his senior civil service colleague. Names like Sir Christopher Bullock, Sir Arthur Street, the wartime PUS who worked so effectively with Portal, and Sir Maurice Dean, PUS from 1955 to 1963, come readily to mind, and there were several more.

Nor, while we are recalling such associates, must we forget the political masters with whom all Chiefs have had to work. For many years, when the Air Ministry was a separate Department of State, the RAF had its own Secretary of State, who presided over the Air Council and thus worked very closely with the CAS as his senior RAF adviser. Men such as Philip Cunliffe-Lister, later Lord Swinton, Sir Kingsley Wood and Sir Archibald Sinclair played major roles in the 1930s and 1940s and the CAS of the day had to ensure his Minister's full support if he was to achieve his aims. In the post-war era the political relationships were more complex, for with the strengthening of the central Ministry of Defence, the single-Service Ministers were first down-graded and then eventually replaced entirely by Ministers with responsibilities extending across all three Services. Chiefs of the Air Staff have, of course, done their best to keep in tune with these changes, which now entail maintaining constant ties with the Defence Secretary and several Ministers, and while the recent ones appreciate the value of the new system in ensuring that the nation's defence is planned and directed as a whole they all regret the passing of the days when the RAF had a Minister it could call its own.

This strengthening of the Ministry of Defence has, of course, had another major consequence. Throughout the inter-war and wartime years, and into the middle 1950s, when there was a separate Ministry for each of the three Services, co-ordination was achieved for normal purposes by the Chiefs of Staff Committee, usually presided over by the most senior member, and by several lower level working committees, most notably the Joint Planning Committee. The CAS of the day thus had to deal closely with his Navy and Army opposite numbers and collectively they answered to the Cabinet for the professional conduct of the nation's military affairs. In the late-1950s, however, the situation began to change, with the appointment first of a Chairman of the Chiefs of Staff (Sir William Dickson) and then of a Chief of the Defence Staff. Ever since then CDS, a five-star officer who up to now has previously been one of the single-Service Chiefs, has presided over the Chiefs of Staff Committee, and gradually – as more and more of the Ministry of Defence staffs have been transferred to his direction – his authority has increased. The CAS, however, continues to make an influential contribution to defence policy, programming and resource issues through his membership of the COS Committee and the Financial Planning and Management Group, the two bodies that represent the senior management of today's Ministry of Defence. His powers and responsibilities in the management of the RAF will be extended in April 1991, when the Ministry's "New Management Strategy" is introduced.

The new structure has, of course, opened up a new opportunity for one in three of the Chiefs of Staff. The RAF provided the first Chief of the Defence Staff, Sir William Dickson, albeit for a brief period; the next RAF holder of the post was Sir Charles Elworthy, and three turns later came Sir Andrew Humphrey and his successor, Sir Neil Cameron. In accordance with the now established practice, Elworthy and Cameron were subsequently created Life Peers. Up to the early 1980s it was accepted that the post would rotate between the three Services, but nowadays this automatic rotation is no longer the rule and the selection is made according to the personalities and the circumstances of the time.

This brings us to a further question, the method of appointing Chiefs of the Air Staff, and here it is impossible to be precise; for the most part the deliberations are not written down and such paperwork as exists is rightly treated in confidence. Certainly, however, each Chief has a say in the appointment of his successor, to the extent of being able to make a recommendation, and on some occasions at least a Chief has been able to exercise influence one stage further ahead. In any case the planning of the careers of senior officers takes such matters into consideration, and a number of CASs have been identified as likely runners a good many years previously. The final decision, however, is always made by the appropriate minister, who – while taking account of the recommendation made – is not bound to accept it. There have indeed been at least one or two occasions when the Prime Minister has intervened and had the last say.

Two more general observations are worth making in the light of my conversations with our more recent Chiefs. One is whether a CAS should ever resign. Apart from Trenchard in 1918 none has yet done so but the possibility has certainly crossed the minds of several of them when faced with some major issue of principle. Portal considered doing so in late 1940 over the control of Coastal Command. More recently there was the occasion when the First Sea Lord, Sir David Luce, resigned on losing the battle for the aircraft carriers; had the Navy won on that occasion it would have been for Sir Charles Elworthy to make the decision. He, however, like others was convinced that resignation served no purpose in such situations; it would have no significant effect and would merely lead to someone less prepared being plunged suddenly into the fray. Sir Keith Williamson felt the same over the Heseltine reorganisation in the 1980s. The consensus seems to be that, unless the Chiefs of all three Services feel so strongly about a particular issue that they are prepared to resign en bloc, there is no point: better to soldier on and do what one can to repair the damage.

One might also ask how far if at all a CAS should attempt to influence his successors. There can be no doubt that Lord Trenchard tried to do so, constantly concerned to ensure that the independence of the Service was being preserved and that the strategic air offensive would remain its primary role. All his successors up to the end of the war had to cope with his promptings and his criticisms, so determined was he to ensure that the RAF was not being led astray, and while his interest and support were appreciated not all his advice was sound. There must certainly have been times when its recipients could have wished him to stay quiet. In later years only one CAS attempted to exercise significant influence, and strangely enough it was the man who as a younger officer had worked closely alongside Trenchard and assisted much of his writing: Sir John Slessor. He, as a keen thinker about air power, remained closely interested in the military challenges of the later 1950s and 1960s, and his successors were all subjected to a steady stream of requests for information, coupled with new ideas. Much of what he had to say made good sense and he was always ready to act as an unofficial public spokesman, but the very process of providing him with answers took time, and it was not always easy to remain patient. It is not surprising, therefore, that other past Chiefs have generally been content to stay behind the scenes. They have recognised that each CAS has to face a different set of circumstances and must act as he thinks fit. All have been willing to offer advice, but only if it has been requested. That is surely as it should be.

To conclude this introduction one underlying feature of every CAS's task deserves a word. Throughout its history the Royal Air Force has had to fight for its continued existence as the Third Service, independent of the Royal Navy and the Army. The pressures have been more intense at some times than others, and without doubt they were at their most acute in Trenchard's day. Yet even during World War II there were bids from the other Services for parts of the RAF that, had they succeeded, could have threatened its existence and, by fragmenting the nation's air power, would have weakened it overall. Moreover, there has been repeated sniping right through the post-war years as attempts have been made to reduce defence expenditure, and the case for the independent Air Force has had to be rehearsed and up-dated on innumerable occasions. Of all our Chiefs' many responsibilities this is the one that has provided the most constant theme. It therefore seems to be essential here to pay brief tribute to the one man whose biography does not feature in this book but whose contribution to the independent Air Force was just as significant as those of all who held the office of CAS. I refer to Lieutenant General Sir David Henderson.

It was Henderson who, having qualified to fly in 1911 at the age of 49, commanded the Royal Flying Corps in France in 1914 and later represented it on the Army Council. By 1917 he had no doubt that there must be a united air service under an independent Air Ministry, a view which he stated unequivocally to General Smuts. He then worked on the Air Organization Committee and in 1918 became Vice-President of the Air Council, from which he resigned at the same time as Trenchard. For him there was no further part to play, but as C G Grey wrote in his obituary: "It was he who first among General Officers realised the vital importance of Military Aviation and took the first steps to set up a separate corps to develop the new arm. British air power will always owe its first debt of gratitude to David Henderson". I therefore judge it right to set him alongside the RAF's 22 most senior officers who feature in this book.

Marshal of the Royal Air Force
The Viscount Trenchard

If the name of just one man could be quoted to personify the Royal Air Force, that name would surely be Lord Trenchard. Presiding over his Service for nearly all of its first twelve years, fighting as maybe nobody else could have done to preserve its independence, laying the foundation on which his successors could build, and imbuing it with the spirit of the offensive that to this day has characterised its operations, he has with justice been called "the Father of the Royal Air Force". He himself, however, disliked the term. In his view it rightly belonged to Lieutenant General Sir David Henderson, who had worked success-fully in 1917 to establish the separate Air Force, and as the builder rather than the creator, Trenchard might have preferred Churchill's description of him as "the supreme architect". Yet his direct responsibilities in the field of military aviation spanned a mere 18 years of his remarkably busy life.

Born at Taunton in 1873, Hugh Trenchard was commissioned in the Royal Scots Fusiliers at the age of 20, and having served in India where he won the All India Rifle Shooting Competition and proved himself an outstanding horseman at polo and racing, he was sent to South Africa to fight in the Boer War. After being shot through the lung, seriously wounded and partly paralysed, he went to Switzerland to convalesce and won the beginners' and freshmen's Cresta Run, largely curing his paralysis in the process. On his return to South Africa Lord Kitchener took advantage of his skilled horsemanship and proved powers of leadership by sending him to organise three mounted infantry battalions, and also on an expedition – unsuccessful – to capture the Boer Government. The next ten years he spent in Nigeria, leading expeditions into the unexplored interior, making tracks and bridges, opening up and pacifying the territory which is now known as Biafra, and latterly commanding the South Nigeria Regiment.

In 1912 he was home again as a 39-year-old Major with only one lung and no obvious career ahead of him, so appreciating that the newly-formed Royal Flying Corps might provide new opportunities, he decided to learn to fly. His course at Weybridge on a Maurice Farman lasted 13 days and entailed one hour 14 minutes' flying time. Now qualified to 'wings' standard, he was sent to the Central Flying School at Upavon where – despite being rated 'an indifferent flyer' – his military experience soon led to his being made Deputy to the first Commandant, Captain Godfrey Paine. His work there led to his appointment to command the Military Wing at Farnborough on the outbreak of war, and in November 1914 to his being sent to lead No 1 Wing in France. A mere nine months later he succeeded General Henderson as the General Officer Commanding, Royal Flying Corps, responsible for all British air operations in support of the British Army on the Western Front.

The next two years were a testing time. While this was a period of great expansion, it was also the time when the Fokker scourge caused enormous losses, and it took a leader of great courage to insist that the offensive must be maintained, even though it entailed heavy casualties; his unfortunate refusal to allow parachutes to be worn was but one way of showing that he meant business. Throughout he worked in co-operation with the French air leaders and his close understanding with Sir Douglas Haig reflected his conviction that the RFC must do all in its power to support the Army. Not least of his many concerns were the need for better flying training, which led to Smith-Barry being given the go-ahead to implement his new ideas, and the supply of aircraft, one of the major problems that led the Government to set up the Smuts Committee which proposed the establishment of a separate Royal Air Force.

Trenchard himself, while fully endorsing General Smuts' predictions about the almost boundless potentialities of air power in the future, and believing that an independent Air Force must eventually come about, did not think this was the right moment for such a fundamental change. In a period of crisis on the Western Front, when the RFC was at last winning acceptance from the Army for its growing contribution, he feared that with the resources then available any diversion from the needs of the RFC would lessen the chances of victory, and doubted if a long-range bombing campaign against Germany – another of the arguments being advanced for establishing the new Service – would at that time be justifiable. Later, however, he was to say that Smuts and Henderson had been more far-sighted than he: had the independent RAF not been created in wartime it would have been impossible to do so afterwards.

The Air Ministry that would oversee the new Service was set up in December 1917, and his success in leading the RFC in France made Trenchard the obvious choice to become its first Chief of the Air Staff. He accepted the summons with considerable reluctance, and his apprehensions about working with the new Air Minister, Lord Rothermere, were quickly confirmed. Such were the differences between them that Trenchard felt obliged to tender his resignation in March 1918, the announcement being delayed until after the RAF had been established on 1 April. Rothermere himself resigned shortly afterwards, and Sir William Weir, his successor, soon decided to offer Trenchard command of the Independent Force based near Nancy, with a view to expanding it into a joint Anglo-French-American bombing force for use in a strategic air offensive against Germany during 1919. Over the next six months, with the Allied Armies at last moving back to the offensive, his bombers attacked a variety of German targets mainly west of the Rhine, their chief purpose being to weaken the will to resist, and preparations went ahead for raids on more distant targets, including Berlin. The Armistice came before much could be achieved, but Trenchard – originally far from enthusiastic about diverting resources from the RFC – had had time to show that strategic bombing might one day prove a weapon of incalculable importance.

The end of the war left him without a job, but early in 1919, when Churchill was appointed Secretary of State for War and Air, Weir advised him to bring back Trenchard as his Chief of the Air Staff. In the post-war situation, few resources would be available for the Air Force and General Sykes, who had replaced Trenchard the previous April, was not thought the right man in such circumstances. In Weir's view, Trenchard could "make do with little and would not have to be carried". Churchill agreed, and for the next ten years it was Trenchard who presided over the fortunes of the Royal Air Force and imprinted his own personality upon it.

In the atmosphere of 1919, when the nation at large wished to put the war behind it and money for defence was scarce, there were many – not least in the Navy and Army – who regarded the infant RAF as an expensive and unnecessary luxury, and it took courage to decide that the new Service, in order to survive, must have its own foundations rather than share those of the older Services, even if this meant a smaller front line. The Central Flying School was already in existence; the other great training institutions of the RAF, notably the Cadet College at Cranwell, the Apprentice School at Halton and the Staff College at Andover, were all founded within Trenchard's first few years; the Short Service Commission Scheme for pilots was introduced in 1919; and in 1925 the first Auxiliary Squadrons and University Air Squadrons were formed. The young Service needed too its raison d'être: if it merely set its sights on 'providing chauffeurs' for the Navy and Army it was doomed, and Trenchard insisted that his Force must concentrate on developing the skills of airmanship as the means of profoundly altering the strategy of the future. In his often quoted Memorandum of December 1919, he therefore made it clear that the main portion of the Air Service would be an independent force, with small parts specifically trained to work with the Navy and Army.

Inevitably, and especially at a time when resources were tight, the older Services were far from content with this, and for most of his time as CAS, particularly the early years, Trenchard fought a series of Whitehall battles either to preserve the RAF as a whole, or to prevent the return of the Naval Air Arm to the Royal Navy. The Balfour Report of 1921, the Geddes Economy Review of 1922, the Salisbury Committee of 1923: these and other inquiries all came down on the side of the RAF, with Geddes, for example, stressing how impressed he was with its economical administration and pointing out that a separate Air Force could better exploit the fast-developing technology. Reflecting on those days, Marshal of the Royal Air Force Sir William Dickson, who served on Trenchard's staff, considered that: "but for his conviction and strength of character, the Air Force would probably not have survived".

Mere theoretical arguments about the indivisibility of the air, however, would not have won the day. While the older Services had their long-proven peace-keeping roles, the RAF had still to convince the sceptics that it could offer value for money, and in the early 1920s Trenchard was quick to seize the opportunity to demonstrate what his aircraft could do. Briefly in British Somaliland and then on a much larger scale in Iraq, the RAF took over the Army's colonial policing role and showed that by exploiting the speed and flexibility of air power, it could do the work far more economically. Thus it was that for most of the inter-war years, a large proportion of the RAF's squadrons were based overseas, carrying out many different types of operations and establishing their reputation alongside the other Services. Meanwhile at home, the annual Hendon air displays demonstrated the quality of RAF flying and by capturing the public's imagination helped to make them air-minded.

So by 1930, when Trenchard handed over to Sir John Salmond, the main battles for the young Service were won, and its unity had been preserved. True, he had not always been successful; for instance after two years of argument he accepted the installation of the first three of six 15" guns to defend the Naval Base at Singapore, since he could not prove that torpedo-carrying aircraft offered the better solution. Perhaps, too, he overestimated the power of the bomber; in forthrightly setting out the doctrine of strategic air power that lay at the heart of the RAF's thinking, he could not have foreseen that the invention of radar would cause the technological balance to swing back at least temporarily towards the defence. In the event, the RAF was to win its first great battle in the defensive role, but as the historian Sir Arthur Bryant was later to write: "we could not have survived and won the war without the RAF's victory in 1940 and without Trenchard's life of service that victory would not have been won".

Now aged 57, Lord Trenchard (as he had just become) still had much to offer the nation, and evidence of his stature may be found in the decision to appoint him Metropolitan Police Commissioner at a time when the reputation of the Police was low and their very loyalty in some doubt. During his four years in that post he had to overcome much antagonism, and not all his reforms were to last; many did, however, and the Police Service owed him much. Thereafter, while he was to devote much of his time to the United Africa Company, the increasing prospect of war led him often to air his views in public, his repeated warnings about the RAF's state of readiness not always endearing him to his successors. When war came he turned himself virtually into an unofficial Inspector-General, travelling extensively both at home and abroad to visit RAF units and spread encouragement and advice, but no more formal role could be found for him and he continued then and for the rest of his life to propound his ideas about the future of air power to all who would listen. He died in 1956 and is buried in Westminster Abbey, in the Battle of Britain Chapel.

Five years later, the Prime Minister, Mr Harold Macmillan, unveiled a Memorial Statue in Whitehall Gardens to the man to whom the nation owed "a debt beyond measure". To Sir Arthur Bryant, he was the greatest leader of men he had ever known. To the American airmen who knew him he was "the patron saint of air power". To the Royal Air Force, he was simply "Boom", the name which somehow exemplified not just his way of speaking, but his total personality. To Maurice Baring, one of his closest colleagues, "he was one of the few big men of the world".

Major General
Sir Frederick Sykes

The Royal Air Force was but a few days old when General Sykes took over from General Trenchard as Chief of the Air Staff. He held the post for less than a year, yet during his term of office he presided over an Air Force that possessed 22,000 aircraft, that had in its ranks 290,000 personnel, and that played a major role in the closing stages of the First World War. His personal contribution in these early days has tended to be obscured amid the conflicts of personalities and the political and economic circumstances of the time but he certainly deserves a full share of the credit for setting the Royal Air Force on course.

Born in Croydon in 1877, Frederick Sykes enlisted as a trooper soon after the outbreak of the Boer War before being commissioned into Lord Roberts' Bodyguard. In 1901, after being seriously wounded, he was granted a regular commission in the 15th Hussars and later, apart from a brief spell in West Africa, served mainly in India, where he attended the Staff College at Quetta in 1908. By now he was developing a growing interest in aviation; indeed as early as 1904 he had taken a course with the Balloon Section of the Royal Engineers, and in June 1911, having started flying lessons at Brooklands the previous year, he was awarded his pilot's certificate flying a Bristol Boxkite. Since he was now filling a staff appointment in the War Office and had become a firm believer in the importance of aerial reconnaissance if war should come, he was a natural choice to join the Sub-Committee of the Committee of Imperial Defence that in 1912 recommended the formation of the Royal Flying Corps, whereupon he was selected to recruit, train and command the Military Wing at Farnborough. The next two years, as he later wrote, were among the happiest and busiest of his life. Amid a general attitude of scepticism, the new Corps had to acquire its aircraft, learn how to maintain and fly them, carry out trials and manoeuvres, and publicise its activities – all at a time when the prospects of war were looming ever larger.

The RFC whose first squadrons went to France on the outbreak of war in August 1914 was therefore largely his creation, but since he was not senior enough to command the force General Sir David Henderson was given the top post with Sykes as his Chief of Staff. For the next nine months Sykes either worked for Henderson or at times stood in for him, but as the Corps rapidly expanded there was increasing debate between those, including Sykes, who believed it should remain centrally controlled and others including Trenchard – now in charge of one of the wings – who thought its units should be under corps or divisional commanders. It was the increasing strains caused by these differences of philosophy, taken together with the incompatibility of two strongly contrasting personalities, that led to Sykes being transferred elsewhere in May 1915.

His destination was Gallipoli, where the Navy had for the time being abandoned its attempt to force the Dardanelles by sea, and the troops that had landed on the beaches were being held by the Turks amid scenes of appalling carnage. Sykes found that the Royal Naval Air Service was doing its best to provide air support though with meagre resources, and after first advising on how to improve matters he was loaned to the Admiralty to command the air forces in the Eastern Mediterranean; these he directed with considerable success in co-operation with the Fleet. When he returned to England in March 1916 he spent the next two years organising the Machine Gun Corps, working on manpower planning in the War Office, and next serving with the British section of the Anglo-French Supreme War Council in Versailles under General Wilson, responsible for manpower, materiel, transport and supplies.

Then, to his great surprise, he was promoted in April 1918 to Major General in order to take over from Trenchard as Chief of the Air Staff. Sharp differences between members of the recently formed Air Council had led Trenchard to resign and Sykes was in no easy situation when charged with the leadership of the newly independent Royal Air Force at a critical point in the war. A staunch believer in the need for a separate Air Force, he quickly set himself to amalgamate the Royal Flying Corps and the Royal Naval Air Service and to set up an independent force for strategic bombing, which he saw as the means of breaking the impasse of trench warfare. The war was to end before this strategy could be put properly to the test, and he almost certainly over-rated its capabilities; nevertheless in his concept lay the seeds of the Bomber Offensive of the Second World War.

It was now time to turn to the problems of peace, and as leader of the British Air Section at the Versailles Peace Conference his main concerns were with enemy disarmament and the organisation of an international air code, where he pressed unsuccessfully for an open skies policy. Meanwhile he had been considering the future structure of the air service; firmly persuaded that air power would now have a world-wide role he envisaged a series of permanent bases throughout the Empire from which an Imperial Striking Force would be deployed, backed up by a reserve of commercial aircraft and all directed by an Imperial Air Staff. To fulfil this concept he proposed in December 1918 an RAF of 62 service and 92 cadre squadrons, plus a further 37 cadre squadrons from the Dominions. When this ambitious scheme was rejected as too costly his alternative proposal was for a home air force of 62 squadrons with civil aviation opening up the Imperial possibilities. In due course this too was turned down and when Churchill was appointed Minister for War and Air in February 1919 he was advised by Sir William Weir, his predecessor as Air Minister, that Trenchard would be better able than Sykes to preserve the RAF with the minimal resources that were likely to be available. Seen with the benefit of hindsight Sykes' ideas appear far-sighted, but to his contemporaries they were out of tune with the national mood and the constraints of economy.

Still aged only 41, Sykes was now appointed Controller-General of Civil Aviation, continuing to work within the Air Ministry but as a civilian. Over the next three years he was closely concerned with producing the new Civil Flying Regulations, organising the meteorological reporting system, planning the Empire air routes, and establishing the International Commission of Aerial

Navigation. In 1922, however, he resigned, feeling that the limited funds provided for his small department gave too little scope for the growth of British civil aviation that he believed would be so important in the future. He now decided to enter the House of Commons, where he used his position to urge the cause of both military and civil flying, as well as extending his interests in other directions, such as by becoming Chairman of the Broadcasting Committee. Then in 1928 he was sworn of the Privy Council and appointed Governor of Bombay, where he spent five very busy years at a time of great turmoil in India. Between 1933 and 1940 he became involved with such organisations as the Miners' Welfare Commission, the Royal Empire Society and the British Sailors' Society, and he spent the wartime years once again as a Member of Parliament. He died in 1954.

To the Royal Air Force he is little known, for the dominant influence over the Service in its earlier years was undoubtedly that of Trenchard. There was little love lost between them. Yet without question General Sykes played an important part in getting first the RFC and then the RAF under way. A born staff officer and organiser, well at home in the corridors of power, he unfortunately did not always hit it off with some of his brother officers, and has certainly received less credit than was his due as one of the main founders of the Royal Air Force.

Marshal of the Royal Air Force
Sir John Salmond

If Sir John Salmond is less widely remembered as a Chief of the Air Staff than he should be this is possibly because he was inevitably over-shadowed by Trenchard, his predecessor, and also because in the early 1930s most of the nation's leaders were obsessed with the search for a formula for disarmament. His earlier achievements, however, make it abundantly clear that he was the right man to take over in 1930, and it was no fault of his that the RAF could do little more than mark time under his direction.

Born in 1881 John Salmond joined the Army in 1900 and after graduating from Sandhurst served first in South Africa and then in the West African Frontier Force. Stationed mainly at home from 1907 onwards he quickly became interested in the military possibilities of flying; having written on 'airships and aeroplanes in war' as one of his annual essay subjects – a duty in those days – he first flew as a passenger at Hendon in 1910 and passed his flying test on a Grahame White biplane in 1912. On secondment to the Royal Flying Corps he was sent to Upavon, where he quickly proved himself an able pilot and a skilled instructor, and in December 1913 flying a BE biplane he set the solo British altitude record of 13,140 feet.

He was obviously a good choice to command 3 Squadron when it went to France on the outbreak of war and, equipped with varied types of aircraft, became engaged mainly on reconnaissance duties. April 1915 saw him back home at Farnborough in command of the RFC training wing, but a mere four months later he returned to the Western Front, this time to lead 2 Wing under Trenchard at a time when the RFC was beginning to suffer heavy losses. It soon became clear that many of the replacement pilots reaching the front-line squadrons were grossly undertrained, and in 1916 Salmond was again sent back to England, this time to reorganise the whole flying training system. A busy year followed, during which many more flying schools were opened, the aircraft supply system improved, minimum training standards laid down and new methods of instruction introduced. In all these activities Salmond was personally involved, flying many of the aircraft himself and often testing new types.

His next change of appointment came in October 1917 when at the remarkably young age of 36 he joined the Army Council, replacing Henderson as Director General of Military Aeronautics. By this time planning was well under way to form the Royal Air Force and when Trenchard came home in January to become the first Chief of the Air Staff it was Salmond who succeeded him in France as Commander of the RFC and then the RAF, whose men he had done so much to train. With some 63 squadrons at his disposal, he now found himself at the centre of the action throughout the German offensive of early 1918 and the Allied counter-offensive that followed. Despite very heavy losses, Salmond's airmen played a major part in reconnoitring and hampering the enemy advance and later in supporting the Allied drive that eventually brought the war to an end, and it was entirely fitting that he should command the RAF contingent in the subsequent Victory Parade.

Still aged only 38 and having already been the RAF's leading field commander, John Salmond clearly had an important future ahead of him. His first post-war command was at Headquarters Inland Area, Uxbridge, where among other things he organised the first Air Pageant at Hendon in 1920, one of whose purposes was to raise money for the recently instituted RAF Benevolent Fund of which he became a life-long supporter. Then in 1922 he went to India to investigate the alleged inefficiency of the RAF and carried out what John Slessor, who had been there at the time, later described as a 'thorough and searching enquiry'. Not one to mince words, Salmond was highly critical of the poor material support being provided by the Army, and stated that the RAF in India was to all intents and purposes non-existent as a fighting force. While his recommendations led to much improvement, he himself was not destined to remain in India. Instead he was to go the the Middle East.

In 1921 the controversial decision had been taken to make the RAF responsible for the internal security of Iraq, where the high cost of the Army garrison was causing great concern. By relying largely on aircraft and RAF-manned armoured cars, Trenchard had argued, Iraq could be effectively policed at far less cost, and on 1 October 1922 Salmond was appointed the first AOC. He took over at a bad moment. The Turks were threatening the northern province of Mosul and a Kurdish rebellion led by Sheik Mahmud was under way, and Salmond's task was made no easier by the lack of firm political direction from the United Kingdom. Nevertheless, by judicious use of bombing and by moving his ground troops quickly forward by air he was able to use his limited resources to restore order in the endangered areas – the first major demonstration of the system of air control that was to be of such value in the inter-war years. It was, according to Maurice Dean, a tremendous victory secured by Salmond's masterly handling.

Having returned home in 1924 he served initially on Trenchard's staff in the Air Ministry, but 1925 saw his appointment as AOCinC Air Defence of Great Britain where he was effectively in charge of the operational Air Force in the United Kingdom for the next three years. This was a difficult time. While the fight for the independent Service was now essentially won, resources were scarce and the RAF was still equipped largely with aircraft of World War I vintage. Its basic doctrine, in which Salmond firmly believed, was that since there was no way of fully defending one's country against air attack, the main weight of the Air Force must be committed to strategic bombing of the enemy's main centres of military preparation, and – surprisingly in retrospect – the potential enemy was perceived as France. There were, of course, plenty of day to day tasks to keep him occupied and in 1928 he visited Australia and New Zealand to advise on the future development of their Air Forces. Then in January 1929 he became Air Member for Personnel, a post he was to fill for exactly a year.

There could hardly have been any question when Trenchard announced his decision to retire on 31 December 1929 that John Salmond would be chosen to replace him. All his achievements and experience pointed to his becoming CAS, and he was a highly skilled and practised pilot. Age too was on his side: he was not yet turned 50. Sadly, however, the circumstances of the time were against his achieving the success in office that this background promised. Nor did it help that Trenchard – certain to be a difficult man to follow – had just called strongly for the RAF to substitute for the older Services in further areas overseas, thus keeping alive the suspicions that had always dogged the RAF's relationships with them.

It was, however, largely external factors that precluded John Salmond from making the impact upon air policy that he must have wanted. The early 1930s were the height of the Great Depression when public resources for all purposes, not least defence, were bound to be hard to come by. They were also years in which the politicians of most nations, determined to avoid a repetition of the mass slaughter of World War I but aware of the continuing tensions in the world, sought to build on the Kellogg-Briand Pact of 1928, which had renounced war as an instrument of policy, and to find a solution in the panacea of total disarmament. Not least of their anxieties was the prospect of aerial bombing. Many of them were convinced this would have appalling consequences in a future war, and in the Geneva Disarmament Conference, which began in 1932 under the auspices of the League of Nations and continued until 1934, there were interminable discussions around proposals to abolish bombing and indeed to abolish military aircraft. While the disarmament negotiations eventually foundered after Hitler came to power in 1933, they had dominated much of the thinking of the government, the press and the public about defence, and John Salmond had had to devote much of his attention to proving the impracticability of what was being proposed, making himself unpopular with the government in the process. As he himself wrote in 1932, "we are in one for the biggest crises in our history, for the other two Services have attacked us through the Disarmament Conference and recommended the total abolition of aerial bombing – I am fighting this tooth and nail". Moreover there were direct effects on the RAF: not only did it have to continue with equipment that was increasingly out-dated but the repeated questioning of its raison d'être in the press both depressed morale and discouraged recruiting. Consequently Britain's air strength fell steadily behind that of countries like France, the USSR, the USA and Italy, whose governments seemed to take more realistic attitudes. To make matters even worse, the loss of the airship R101 in 1930, with the Air Minister and Minister of Civil Aviation on board, was a blow to Britain's aviation pride from which it was not easy to recover.

All, however, was not gloom. Despite the lack of public finance, it was the RAF that won outright the Schneider Trophy in 1931, thus setting firmly on course the line of development that would lead to the Spitfire. Planning was also set in train for some of the aircraft with which the RAF would enter the war; the specification for the Wellington, for example, was issued in 1932. But it is hard to reflect on the Salmond years without sympathy for a man whose qualities would under almost any other circumstances have been far better used, and whose retirement on 31 March 1933 came at a time when no leader of the RAF could have been popular.

He was to have been succeeded by his elder brother Geoffrey, who held very similar views on the importance of air power in any future war and had been openly critical of those who wished to abolish the RAF. Geoffrey Salmond, who had earlier fought in South Africa and China, had joined the RFC in 1912; in the early months of the war he had served on Henderson's staff in France and then commanded 1 Squadron: the remainder of the war he had spent mainly in the Middle East ending up as AOC, a post he retained until 1922. He had later been Air Member for Supply and Research on the Air Council, AOC India at the time of the Kabul Airlift, and AOCinC Air Defence of Great Britain. Sadly, however, though appointed to succeed his brother on 1 April 1933, he became ill before he could take over and died a month later. Consequently John Salmond stood in for him until another successor could be selected, and this time the choice fell upon Sir Edward Ellington.

Much of Sir John Salmond's time from now on was devoted to duties as a Director of Imperial Airways but he remained in close touch with his old Service and when war came his talents and experience were put to use first in the Ministry of Aircraft Production and later the Air Ministry as Director General of Flying Control and Air Sea Rescue. One of his most significant tasks was to chair in 1940 the committee which investigated the performance of the night air defences. Though ill health forced his retirement in 1943, he was to continue for many years as a father figure of the RAF who could be counted upon to appear at any major RAF function, and he took an interest in many of its activities, such as the RAF Club of which he was President for 23 years. He died in 1968, aged 87. It had been his misfortune as CAS to have to preside over the RAF during what Churchill described as 'the locust years'. Perhaps his greatest contributions to the Royal Air Force came earlier, notably in Iraq in 1923/24 and on the Western Front in 1918. In the words of Maurice Dean: "It was Trenchard and John Salmond who, by their special qualities of leadership in dreadful days in France, impressed the fighting service of the air with a stamp and quality which it has never lost".

Marshal of the Royal Air Force
Sir Edward Ellington

Sir Edward Ellington, who would never have become Chief of the Air Staff but for the untimely death of Sir Geoffrey Salmond, has all too often received a bad press. Possessed of a cautious, somewhat retiring nature, he may not have been the most inspiring leader, yet as John Terraine remarks, "his 4½ years saw a veritable transformation of the RAF", and if a man is to be judged by his achievements Ellington's place in RAF history is safe.

Compared with most of his RAF contemporaries his background was unusual. Commissioned into the Royal Artillery in 1897 at the age of 20, he graduated from the Staff College ten years later and then went to the War Office; it was while serving there that he obtained his pilot's licence in 1912. Having completed his staff tour first by serving as Secretary to Henderson's Royal Flying Corps Planning Committee and afterwards by heading the air policy and administrative section of the newly formed Military Aeronautics Directorate, he next moved to Upavon where he qualified as a military pilot in December 1913.

Strangely his newly acquired skills were not to be used: instead he returned to normal staff and regimental duties and spent most of the First World War in France, not with the RFC but with the Royal Artillery. Apart from a brief interlude in 1916 when he joined Henderson in representing the War Office on Lord Derby's Joint War Air Committee, it was November 1917 before he was to be further involved with military aviation, and again it was his staff skills that were in demand when he was appointed Deputy to the Director General of Military Aeronautics, John Salmond. A mere two months later, when Salmond returned to France, it was Ellington who succeeded him, and in August 1918 he joined the recently formed Air Council as Controller General of Equipment, a post that was subsequently redesignated Director General of Supply and Research. Thus it was that for the first three peacetime years Ellington found himself working alongside Trenchard in establishing the structure of the young Royal Air Force and resolving its many day-to-day problems.

There followed seven years abroad, as Air Officer Commanding first in the Middle East, then in India and finally in Iraq. These tours of duty gave him extensive experience of operational command at a time when much of the active flying of the RAF was taking place overseas, and his squadrons were regularly engaged in peace-keeping operations – notably against the Mahsuds on the North West Frontier in 1925, against Sheikh Mahmud in Kurdistan in 1927, and against incursions along the south-west frontier of Iraq in 1928. By the time he left at the end of that year the RAF was able to control Iraq with a remarkably small force; the eight squadrons needed in the earlier 1920s were soon to be reduced to five and of 33 British and Indian army battalions stationed there in 1921 the last was just being withdrawn.

1929 saw Ellington back at home, having survived an air crash on the way.

1 *Major-General Hugh Trenchard – a First World War portrait.*

2 *An informal moment during the Second World War: Lord Trenchard and Sir Arthur Tedder.*

3 *A serious conversation with Her Majesty the Queen, always a great supporter of the Royal Air Force. Princess Margaret is on the left.*

4 *At his funeral in Westminster Abbey in 1956, the Royal Air Force pays tribute to Lord Trenchard. Among the pall-bearers are Lord Portal, Lord Douglas, Lord Newall, Lord Tedder and Sir Arthur Harris.*

5 *Major-General Sir Frederick Sykes with his colleagues in the British Air Section at the Peace Conference in Paris, February 1919. Seated on his right is Colonel P R C Groves, the Air Adviser to the British Ambassador, and on his left is Mr H White-Smith, representing civil aviation. Back row (left to right): Captain Crosbie, Captain Tindal-Atkinson, an unidentified Major, Colonel Blandy, Captain Lyall.*

6 *Major-General Frederick Sykes – a First World War portrait.*

7 *Sir Frederick Sykes in later life.*

8 The Dinner to mark the 40th Anniversary of the Royal Air Force, held at Stanmore Park on 1 April 1958. Seated at the top table with members of the Royal Family are, from left to right, Lord Douglas, Lord Newall, the Rt Hon George Ward, Sir Dermot Boyle, Sir John Salmond and Lord Tedder.

9 Sir John Salmond visits RAF Upwood on 9 October 1963 to present its Sovereign's Standard to 7 Squadron. On his left is the Station Commander, Group Captain Carter.

10 On 18 May 1962 Sir John Salmond, the Senior Marshal of the RAF, lays his wreath at the Cenotaph during the Ceremony to mark the 50th Anniversary of the formation of the Royal Flying Corps.

11 Six Marshals of the RAF ride in the Queen's Coronation Procession in 1953. In the leading coach are Sir Arthur Harris, Sir John Slessor, Lord Tedder and Lord Douglas; following them are Sir John Salmond and Sir Edward Ellington.

12 Marshal of the Royal Air Force Sir Edward Ellington, a signed portrait.

13 Sir Edward Ellington at Alexandria, about to board SS PODESTA for Constantinople, 1922.

14 Sir Edward Ellington (third from left) with Sir Samuel Hoare and others at Hinaidi, 1926.

15 Sir Cyril Newall, carrying his gas mask and official papers, 1939.

16 Sir Cyril Newall inspecting an aircraft in France in December 1939, watched by Air Commodore Lord Londonderry (Air Minister in the early 1930s) and Air Vice-Marshal Playfair, Commander of the Advanced Air Striking Force.

17 The Air Council in session at the Air Ministry, in July 1940. Left to right: Air Marshal A G R Garrod (Air Member for Training), Sir Harold Howitt (Additional Member), Air Marshal Sir Christopher Courtney (AMSO), Air Marshal E L Gossage (AMP), Captain H H Balfour (US of S for Air), The Rt Hon Sir Archibald Sinclair (Secretary of State for Air), Air Chief Marshal Sir Cyril Newall (CAS), Sir Arthur Street (PUS), Air Chief Marshal Sir Wilfrid Freeman (Air Member for Development and Production), Sir Charles Craven (Civil Member for Development and Production), Mr R H Melville (Private Secretary to S of S), Flight Lieutenant W W Wakefield MP (Parliamentary Private Secretary). Air Marshal Sir Richard Peirse (VCAS) was not present on this occasion.

After a period in command of Air Defence of Great Britain where he was responsible for all the bomber and fighter squadrons based in the United Kingdom, together with their supporting units, in September 1931 he rejoined the Air Council, this time as Air Member for Personnel. Thus by April 1933, when he was selected to become Chief of the Air Staff, he had held virtually all the top level command and staff appointments in the RAF. Yet incredibly he had done no operational flying himself and had never commanded a squadron, wing or group, and it is therefore hardly surprising that in some quarters his appointment was viewed with misgivings. On the other hand, C G Grey, Editor of "Aeroplane", considered that "with such all-round modern experience (including much passenger flying as an AOC while overseas) none could be better fitted for the high responsible position he now held".

The challenge he faced was formidable. His predecessor, John Salmond, through no fault of his own had been able to do little more than maintain the fabric of the Service in face of the demands for economy and the pressures for disarmament, and Ellington inherited an Air Force comprising no more than 30,000 personnel and equipped mainly with aircraft that were long out-of-date. For much of his first year the Disarmament Conference at Geneva meandered on, considering such ideas as an international air pact whose signatories would promise never to bomb each other, but with Hitler now in power in Germany and beginning to rearm, the British government started to realise it would need to do likewise. For the RAF the initial decision was to complete the programme for a Home Defence Force of 52 squadrons (originally announced in 1923), and soon afterwards in July 1934 the first of a series of expansion plans, Scheme A, postulated a force of 75 squadrons for home defence by 1939. Ellington has been criticised for not pressing the RAF case even more strongly at this time, but the habits of so many lean years were not easy to discard, and he himself doubted if Germany could be ready for war before 1942. In any event, as he was at pains to stress, over-rapid expansion would not only cause the accumulation of large numbers of obsolete or obsolescent aircraft but present grave problems in recruiting and training the many aircrew and technical tradesmen that would be needed; if the quality and efficiency of the Service were to be preserved, expansion would have to be carefully controlled. Politically too, this approach made sense: as the Peace Ballot conducted by the League of Nations Union in June 1935 showed, pacifism still had many adherents, and an over-emphasis on rearmament might well have cost Prime Minister Stanley Baldwin the general election that came soon afterwards.

1936, however, was another story. Now the political issue was settled and the military argument was less about the reality of the German threat than its extent. Scheme F, the only one of the many expansion schemes actually to be fulfilled in the planned timescale, was approved in February; essentially it was intended to provide by March 1939 some 124 squadrons in the United Kingdom, 26 in the Fleet Air Arm and 37 overseas. Most significantly, and reflecting the conviction of Ellington and many of his colleagues that the fighter could not defend successfully against the bomber, the ratio between bombers and fighters would be 5:2. Planning for the Wellington and Whitley heavy bombers would continue unchanged, and the Harts, Hinds and Gordons of the current light bomber force would be replaced by Hampdens, Blenheims and Battles, classified as mediums. Of these the Battle in particular came in later for much criticism, yet at the time there was no real alternative if the RAF was to bridge the gap until the next generation of bombers could appear. Nevertheless, the planning for these was also in train, for in 1936 were issued the specifications that eventually led to the building of the real heavy bombers of World War II: the Stirling, the Halifax and the Lancaster.

But if Ellington and some of his staff were sceptical about the practicalities of air defence, they still presided over a series of advances that a few years later would lead to victory in the Battle of Britain. In 1934 specifications were issued for new monoplane fighter aircraft: the Hurricane and Spitfire that were then designed first flew in 1935 and 1936 respectively and were immediately ordered in quantity. In 1935 the Committee for the Scientific Survey of Air Defence, chaired by Henry Tizard, directed a series of successful experiments in radio direction finding which led to the development of the radar system that would provide the key to successful air defence. In 1936 the all-embracing structure known as Air Defence of Great Britain was superseded by new functional commands entitled Bomber, Fighter, Coastal and Training, thus instituting the organisational framework within which World War II would be fought. Later that year the decision was taken to form a new RAF Volunteer Reserve, wherein a great many part-time airmen would learn to fly. Meanwhile a major airfield building programme was under way: the 52 home airfields of 1934 became 89 in 1938. Furthermore, to meet the likely need for far more aircraft, a scheme for shadow factories was introduced, purchasing procedures were improved, and plans were started to buy aircraft from the USA.

These far-reaching changes, and many more, were of course accomplished by joint effort. Ellington was fortunate to serve under one of the Service's greatest Secretaries of State, Lord Swinton, and among his senior colleagues were a number who would in due course become household names: Cyril Newall, Hugh Dowding, Frederick Bowhill, Christopher Courtney, Wilfrid Freeman, Arthur Harris, Arthur Tedder. He led a remarkably strong team. Nevertheless, while much was achieved, a great deal remained to be done before the RAF as a whole could be considered ready for war. Not the least of its shortcomings were in the spheres of army and naval co-operation, and shortly before his retirement Ellington had to concede control of the Fleet Air Arm to the Royal Navy, a defeat over which he was sternly censured by the ever-watchful Trenchard. Yet such was his standing when he handed over to Sir Cyril Newall on 31 August 1937 that he was immediately appointed Inspector General of the RAF, a post which he retained until he finally retired from active duty in 1940. He travelled the world on his tours of inspection, and throughout the winter months of 1939-40 showed the utmost diligence in his visits to units of every kind. Despite his essential shyness "Uncle Ted", as the Air Force knew him, had come to be held in great affection. Although he continued to appear at major functions his later years were spent away from public duties and he died in 1967.

Maurice Dean, who served as Ellington's Private Secretary for most of his time as CAS and therefore knew him particularly well, appraised him in later years. While accepting that at times it was Ministers rather than he who led the way and that he had little personal knowledge of aviation, Dean was at pains to stress his acute mind, his remarkable memory and his quickness to embrace new ideas. He was in other words a superb staff officer. In the circumstances of the mid-1930s no other quality could have been more important.

Marshal of the Royal Air Force
The Lord Newall

When Sir Cyril Newall took over from Sir Edward Ellington on 1 September 1937, few had much doubt that Britain would sooner or later again be at war with Germany, and the challenge he faced was to build on the work of his predecessors so as to prepare the RAF for a conflict whose timing and pattern were impossible to foretell. Since inevitably many shortcomings were to be revealed under the pressures of war, Newall has come in for his share of criticism, and some have seen the decision to retire him in October 1940, when still aged only 54, as a verdict on his conduct of affairs. Such a view is highly unjust.

Cyril Newall was born in India in 1886; after training at Sandhurst, he was commissioned in the Royal Warwickshire Regiment in 1905 and saw active service against Pathan raiders on the North West Frontier in 1908. The following year he transferred to the 2nd Gurkha Rifles. It was in 1911, while home on leave, that he learnt to fly in a Bristol Biplane at Larkhill, and having gained his RFC 'wings' at the Central Flying School, Upavon, in 1913, he was posted as an instructor at the newly formed Indian CFS at Sitapur.

On the outbreak of war he returned home, first to become a Flight Commander in 1 Squadron and then to lead 12 Squadron and take it to France where, equipped with the BE2c, it took part in the Battle of Loos, bombing railways and carrying out reconnaissance. On one occasion, Newall led a party of airmen to extinguish a fire in a large bomb store, thus preventing a catastrophic explosion and earning himself the Albert Medal, the then equivalent of the George Cross. By the end of 1916, he was directly answerable to Trenchard as Commander of 9 Wing, whose seven squadrons provided the RFC's main long-range bombing and reconnaissance force in France, and his now considerable experience of bombing made him the obvious choice to lead the new 41 Wing in October 1917. Established as part of the countermeasures to the German night bombing of London, 41 Wing was formed with the special object of attacking targets of military importance in German territory, and its three squadrons were based at Ochey, near Nancy in Eastern France. In February 1918 the Wing became VIII Brigade, in May two further squadrons arrived, and by June the force had carried out 142 raids, 57 of them against Germany. With the decision to expand VIII Brigade into the Independent Force under Trenchard, Newall now became his deputy, but the war was over before its hoped-for potential could be achieved.

Highly regarded as a wartime commander, Newall was well placed to share in the direction of the post-war Air Force, and after spending three years in the Air Ministry as Deputy Director of Personnel, he found himself in August 1922 at the recently opened 1 School of Technical Training at Halton, as deputy to the Commandant. The RAF of the future would rely for its technical tradesmen largely on the Apprentices Scheme which was being introduced there, and in his 2½ years at Halton, Newall did much to establish its reputation and ensure its success.

Apart from a few short postings, his next 12 years were spent in three major appointments. Between 1926 and 1931 he served in the Air Ministry as Director of Operations and Intelligence and Deputy Chief of the Air Staff, thus carrying a particularly wide range of responsibilities; from 1931 to 1934 he was in Cairo as AOC Middle East, responsible for the Air Forces in Egypt, Sudan, Palestine and Transjordan; and in January 1935 he was given the newly established appointment of Air Member for Supply and Organisation, thus taking over from Hugh Dowding some of his former duties as Air Member for Supply and Research. So Newall was now back at the centre of affairs for the start of the expansion schemes, with a key role in the organisation and provisioning for the RAF and its building programme.

He had every reason, therefore, not only to understand the progress being made, but also to appreciate the immense amount that still needed to be done when he took over from Ellington as CAS in September 1937. That he was preferred to Dowding and Ludlow-Hewitt, both of whom thought they were in the running, was almost certainly thanks to Lord Swinton, the Secretary of State, but without doubt Newall was amply qualified by his Service experience. Working closely alongside him throughout his term of office was his Director of Plans, John Slessor*, and he – ever one to speak his mind – right at the start briefed Newall that the Home Air Force in general, and Bomber Command in particular, was totally unfitted for war. A mere month later, Swinton and Newall submitted a new expansion scheme – Scheme J – for completion by 1941. Based on a full appreciation of German air strength and intentions, this was designed to maintain parity with the German striking force and thus provide an effective deterrent.

In urging Scheme J, Newall was, of course, holding firm to the traditional doctrine of the RAF that the bomber force was fundamentally the basis of all strategy, and the counter-offensive the most important element in home defence. He was, after all, probably the most highly experienced bomber commander of World War I, and he and his colleagues on the Air Staff, constantly exercised by the possibility of the Germans delivering the "knock-out blow", saw it as their duty not to let the Government forget the danger as they saw it. It therefore came as a major shock when Sir Thomas Inskip, the Minister for Co-ordination of Defence, now challenged their basic philosophy. In his view – and he was in part influenced by financial considerations – the role of the Air Force was not to deliver an early knock-out blow, of which it was incapable, but to prevent the Germans doing so. Consequently, the RAF did not need as many bombers as Germany but the fighter force should be as strong as possible. Swinton, Newall and the Air Staff strongly resisted this inadequate and defeatist approach, as it seemed to them, but the Cabinet supported Inskip and a new Scheme K, which laid much more emphasis on fighter aircraft, had to be accepted. In the event, this was just as well.

The mounting pressure of events now began to tell, for the German annexation of Austria in March 1938 compelled the realisation that war might

* See page 42

be only months away. The problem now, as Newall and Slessor saw it, was whether to press ahead with the longer-term schemes for expansion or to concentrate on bringing the existing forces to readiness, and Newall strongly urged the latter course: constant and rapid increase of the front line was of no use without the complex supporting structure and organisation that would render it fit to go to war. Politically, however, it was now impossible to halt or delay the expansion and yet another new Scheme – L – was proposed by the Air Ministry. This, again, entailed heavier expenditure and when both the Chancellor of the Exchequer and Inskip opposed it, Newall reacted strongly: "the time for mincing words is past . . . no one can say with absolute certainty that a nation can be knocked out from the air, because no one has yet attempted it . . . Germany and Italy believe it possible . . . the issue is that of the survival of British civilisation". The Cabinet heeded his warning and Scheme L went through.

Newall's strong lead showed itself in other ways, not least when he agreed Sir Wilfrid Freeman's proposal in the summer of 1938 to order large-scale production of the three heavy bombers off the drawing board; as Slessor wrote: "if Newall had no other claim to fame, his reputation would rest secure on his having sponsored the programme which ultimately gave us Bomber Command as it developed in the later stages of the war". A few months later, as Maurice Dean remembers: "after Munich, he called his staff together, called it a national humiliation, and said they must work night and day to prepare for the trials that would surely come. No one present ever forgot his words". At the same time, according to Slessor, it was on Newall's initiative that the Chiefs of Staff asked at last to be allowed to discuss plans with the French.

Yet for all the efforts of Newall and his staff, the RAF in 1938 was still in poor shape, and would have been ill-placed if required to fight. Much of the most valuable work that was under way was behind the scenes and with the RAF strength becoming increasingly inferior to the German, the Air Ministry found itself under growing criticism from within as well as outside the Service. Ludlow-Hewitt, for example, was constantly urging the need to remedy the many inadequacies of Bomber Command, and Dowding left nobody in any doubt about the needs of Fighter Command. Newall and his colleagues were now paying for the shortcomings of national policy over earlier years. At the same time, while he showed growing understanding of the importance of air defence and the significance of Radio Direction Finding, he remained firmly opposed to the continental commitment, with the enormous drain on the RAF's resources that Army co-operation would impose.

It was, however, that continental commitment which was to be one of his foremost concerns when war came in September 1939. The RAF was obliged to send to France substantial elements from both Fighter and Bomber Commands, and within days he and the CIGS were across the Channel attempting to ascertain the French plans. He was now, as the longest standing member, Chairman of the Chiefs of Staff Committee, and for the first year of the war acted as their spokesman, often in attendance at Cabinet meetings; both in discussion of longer term planning and at moments of crisis, his wise counsel was of great value.

Such a moment came in May 1940. Having successfully resisted his Navy and Army colleagues' pressure to bomb Germany after the attack on Norway, he realised when Holland and Belgium were invaded that the critical time had come: so far, he urged, the enemy had always seized the initiative, and Britain must now react by bombing the Ruhr. The War Cabinet agreed and the strategic bombing offensive commenced, albeit on much too small a scale to achieve significant success at this stage of the war. Meanwhile, in France, the scale of the land and air fighting and the growing seriousness of the situation threatened to drain away the resources of Fighter Command; while Dowding is rightly credited for his forthright stand, Newall too had no doubts about the need to conserve the home fighter force, and without his consistent and vigorous presentation of the case in the War Cabinet the argument might still have been lost. Thus the stage was set for the Battle of Britain, when the spotlight fell on Dowding and "The Few", but here again the strong support of Newall and his staff was fundamental to the victory.

Then, on 24 October, Newall departed. He had been CAS for over three years, had coped with enormous pressure and much criticism, often ill-informed, both in the lead-up to war and during its first disastrous phases, and understandably the strain was probably beginning to tell. Maurice Dean says quite simply that he was retired in accordance with the honourable tradition that you may not stay for ever. He spent the rest of the war as the highly respected Governor General of New Zealand, and on returning home in 1946 was raised to the peerage. He died in 1963.

Newall has so far been – and hopefully will remain – the only CAS to hold office on the outbreak of a major war, and like many other high commanders in history who have been similarly placed, he had to take a share of the blame for the weaknesses that were revealed under the pressure of conflict. It is certainly possible to argue that he and his staff could have done more in specific areas, but when one considers the enormous range of problems they had to contend with, the intense competition for scarce resources, and the continuing political reluctance to face the inevitability of war, it is unfair to be too critical. John Terraine, while seeing him as too closely wedded to the bomber doctrine, observes that "during his tenure, the RAF's most vigorous pre-war expansion took place" and concludes that "his claim to fame lies chiefly in the manner in which he presided over this feverish and testing period". According to Slessor, who was ideally placed to offer a judgement, and "had seldom met a man who was so good for one's morale", he was "the prime architect of the wartime Air Force". When one remembers that he also presided over the RAF at the time of its greatest victory, then surely his reputation is secure.

Air Chief Marshal
The Lord Dowding

"The only commander who won one of the few decisive battles in history and got sacked for his pains". Thus long afterwards wrote Sir Arthur Harris, one of many both in and outside the RAF who believed that Lord Dowding had been unjustly treated after the Battle of Britain and should have received more ample recognition. As we look back with the benefit of hindsight, it is clear that he should have been created a Marshal of the Royal Air Force, but as Maurice Dean remarks: "It did not look like that at the time".

Hugh Dowding was born in 1882 at Moffat. Educated at Winchester and the Royal Military Academy, Woolwich, he was commissioned in the Royal Garrison Artillery and served first in Gibraltar, Ceylon and Hong Kong and then for six years in India with the Mountain Artillery. There followed two years at the Staff College, Camberley, during which he took the opportunity to learn to fly at Brooklands, and in 1913 he gained his 'wings' at the Central Flying School before being placed in the RFC reserve.

The outbreak of war saw him first at Farnborough and then with 6 and 9 Squadrons in France. His interest in wireless telegraphy led to his returning home to form the Wireless Experimental Establishment at Brooklands in April 1915, but within months he was back in France, this time commanding 16 Squadron whose main role was artillery observation. After a further spell at Farnborough he spent much of 1916 in command of the Ninth (Headquarters) Wing during the Battle of the Somme, but owing to differences of opinion with Trenchard he was then sent to run the Southern Training Brigade at Salisbury, where he remained for the rest of the war.

Despite his wartime advancement to the rank of Brigadier it was only after some delay that he was awarded the permanent RAF commission that he wanted, thus enabling him to join that select band of senior officers who would lay the foundations of the new Service. His first major post at HQ 1 Group, Kenley, included responsibility for some of the early Hendon Air Pageants; he then served as Chief Staff Officer first at HQ Inland Area, Uxbridge and then at HQ Iraq. The significant year, however, was 1926 when he moved to the Air Ministry to become Director of Training. For the first time he was able to influence policy, and his hitherto strained relations with Trenchard now improved to the extent that in 1929 he was appointed AOC Transjordan and Palestine at a time of growing hostility between the Jews and Arabs. There followed a short spell as AOC Fighting Area before he was appointed to the Air Council as Air Member for Supply and Research at the end of 1930.

From now on, first as AMSR and then from 1935 Air Member for Research and Development, the increasingly complex technical matters associated with the building of a modern air force were to be Dowding's prime concern, and although he had no scientific training he was to show a remarkable capacity for understanding them. One of his many activities was to encourage the development of advanced fighter aircraft based on the experience gained in the Schneider Trophy, and it was largely on his initiative that the prototypes for the Hurricane and Spitfire were ordered in 1934. He also showed the closest interest in the research into methods of detecting hostile aircraft, and responded to the success of the early Radio Detection Finding experiments in 1935 by providing every possible support. While his duties ranged far wider than air defence, it was probably in this field that his contributions were most significant, and he was the natural choice to become Commander-in-Chief of the new Fighter Command when it was set up in July 1936.

He had at that time some expectations of succeeding Ellington as CAS and was understandably disappointed when in 1937 the decision went in favour of Newall. The task at Fighter Command was, however, more suited to him – as he himself later recognised – and he was content to be able to continue the supremely important work of preparing his Command for war. Altogether he spent over four years at Bentley Priory, most of them being devoted to creating an intricate and smoothly working system which combined the Fighter Force, the RDF units and the Communications and Control organisations into a structure that was well ahead of anything else in the world. To do so, however, he had to keep what he saw as an obstructive Air Ministry under constant pressure as he urged improvement upon improvement. Bullet-proof windscreens for his fighters, the installation of IFF, the construction of hard runways, the building of proper operations rooms, the development of the Observer Corps, the introduction of an air raid warning system: these were but a few of the countless matters that engaged him and his staff. Finally, to complete the system, on the outbreak of war he was given operational control of Anti-Aircraft Command and Balloon Command.

Yet for all that had been achieved Dowding had deep anxieties as war approached. Notwithstanding the greater priority accorded to fighter production from 1938 onwards, his fighter strength – as he regularly pointed out to higher authority – was far from adequate for the proper defence of the homeland, and it was increasingly clear that when the Army went to France some of his Hurricanes would have to go with it. For him, totally convinced that the security of the home base must come before all else and that this rested upon the twin pillars of Fighter Command and the Royal Navy, the all too likely prospect of having his fighters drained away in France was intolerable.

The moment of truth came on 15 May 1940 when, after five days of intense fighting on the Continent, he urged on the War Cabinet the dire consequences should the present rate of wastage continue. The letter Dowding wrote the next day is one of the great documents of history. It concludes: "If the Home Defence Force is drained away in desperate attempts to remedy the situation in France, defeat in France will involve the final, complete and irremediable defeat of this country". It was this unequivocal statement that first set out the stark alternatives, yet the debate on sending more fighters was not to be finally resolved for almost another month, during which time Dowding would see his resources "slipping away like sand in an hour-glass" – not least during the air fighting to cover the Dunkirk evacuation, when as Churchill saw it Dowding won the RAF's first victory over the Luftwaffe. Nevertheless, serious as his losses were, they were not mortal. He had retained just enough of his aircraft to enable him in due course to fight the Luftwaffe in the one place where they could be effectively used, within the comprehensive air defence system he had built up in the United Kingdom. Maurice Dean recalls Dowding's visit to the Air Staff Secretariat at the time of the French collapse. His face shone as he spoke: "Now we cannot lose".

Even so, as he himself later admitted in his despatch, the situation he faced in the Battle of Britain was "critical in the extreme". While it is indisputable that the immortal "Few" – his chicks as Churchill called them – won the Battle using the organisation he had created, it is equally true that the Luftwaffe lost it through bad senior leadership, faulty tactics and mistaken target selection. But as always the victory is what matters, and Dowding, who saw his aim quite simply as to prevent a German invasion by denying them control of the air, did just that. His personal role was, of course, limited. The overall deployment and rotation of his squadrons, the maintenance of reserves of aircraft and pilots, the planning of night defences; matters such as these were his concern but subject to his general directives the control of the actual fighting was a matter for his Group Commanders.

In the key positions were Keith Park at 11 Group, whose personality and views matched closely those of Dowding, and Trafford Leigh-Mallory at 12 Group, who was far less sympathetic. The differences between these two, not least over the latter's questionable employment of 'big wings', became increasingly marked as the Battle progressed, and Dowding, ensconced for most of the time in his own Headquarters, seemed unaware of them. As Robert Wright quotes him: "What I did not know was that Leigh-Mallory's conduct as a whole amounted to a challenge to my orders". But, to echo Maurice Dean, it is a serious criticism that he failed to settle the squabble between the two Groups: "Commanders have to know".

Now aged 58, embarrassingly senior to the rest of the RAF's high commanders, under formidable strain and increasingly remote from those he led, Dowding was being widely criticised. At the Air Ministry, where the more aggressive but untried policies favoured by Leigh-Mallory were preferred, he was seen as a non-cooperator, a man with whom it was difficult to get on, and in contrast to Fighter Command's success in the daylight battle, the Luftwaffe seemed to be having its own way in the night offensive. Unfair as it now seems to blame Dowding for this, there were many who believed it was time for a change. Portal, who was 11 years his junior and had just taken over as CAS, felt that Dowding was not the type of commander needed to lead Fighter Command after the Battle of Britain. Even Churchill, who had told Sinclair, the Secretary of State for Air, in July that he thought Dowding was one of the very best men he had got and who greatly admired the whole of his work in Fighter Command, was eventually persuaded, though as he said, "it broke my heart" to agree, and on 13 November Sinclair met him to convey the news.

While one can under all the circumstances agree with his biographer, Basil Collier, that this decision was not unreasonable, it is very hard to accept the way in which Dowding was treated personally. Since July 1938, when Newall had told him that he would be retired in June 1939, he had been repeatedly invited to extend his service by short periods and on 12 August 1940 he was asked by Newall to remain without time limit. The conviction that the Service did not want him but could not do without him was inescapable. Then, when he was finally moved from Fighter Command, he was persuaded by Churchill, much against his will, to head an aircraft purchasing mission to the USA, a role for which he was quite unsuited and from which he soon had to be withdrawn. A further task allotted to him, a major RAF economy study, proved equally inappropriate and he finally retired in 1942, still an Air Chief Marshal. Certainly, as Slessor said, this was shabby treatment, but the highest rank in the Service had hitherto been reserved exclusively for former Chiefs of the Air Staff, and there was no will among the top leaders of the RAF to break with precedent, even when it was suggested by the King. The peerage Dowding was awarded the following year was thus the one formal recognition of his achievements.

Lord Dowding spent the rest of his life largely away from the Royal Air Force scene, devoting some of his interest to spiritualism and such causes as the prevention of cruelty to animals. Nevertheless as President of the Battle of Britain Fighter Association and a regular attender of its reunions he was always held in great respect and affection by those whom he had led. He died in 1970 and his remains were interred in Westminster Abbey. Delivering the address on this occasion, Denis Healey, the Secretary of State for Defence, summed him up as "One of those great men whom this country miraculously produces in times of peril".

If we today are surprised at the seeming ingratitude of many of Dowding's contemporaries, we must recall that the significance of his contribution was less clear than it is now. The very qualities that had enabled him to build, protect and lead his Command had made him a hard man for others to deal with, and had certainly not helped him fit easily into the team. As Denis Richards wrote of him, until the home base was secure "he proposed neither to understand other arguments, nor to compromise, nor even to accept with good grace the decisions that went against him". Yet while the criticisms of those who knew him and worked with him can be understood, we of a later generation could wish that they had been more generous. For when all is said and done, to use the words of John Terraine: "Dowding goes down in history as the one airman with an indisputable victory in a recognisable battle of decisive importance to his name".

Marshal of the Royal Air Force
The Viscount Portal

Of all Chiefs of the Air Staff, on none did the spotlight shine more strongly than on Sir Charles Portal. Leading his Service for much the largest part of the war and answering directly to perhaps the greatest of all wartime Prime Ministers, he had to carry an enormous strain, and there were few who worked closely with him during those years who did not have the highest regard for his abilities. While he has had his share of latter-day critics, most of them have over-emphasised particular incidents and failed to appreciate the value of his total contribution to the Allied victory.

Peter Portal, as he was always known by his friends, was born in Hungerford in 1893. Intending to qualify eventually as a barrister, he went from school at Winchester to Christ Church, Oxford in 1912, but the war cut short his degree course and on enlisting as a despatch rider in the Royal Engineers, he was sent to France and soon commissioned. Shortly afterwards he was seconded to the Royal Flying Corps in which, without any previous training, he flew operationally with 3 Squadron in 1915 as an Air Observer. Then in May 1916, having spent four months learning to be a pilot, he went back to France, where he flew – mainly on reconnaissance and artillery observation – first with 60 Squadron, then as Flight Commander with 3 Squadron, and from June 1917, as OC 16 Squadron. Such rapid advancement, accompanied by the award of the MC and two DSOs, was a clear tribute to his outstanding qualities, both as pilot and leader, and he was an obvious choice for a permanent commission in the post-war RAF.

He had returned home from France in June 1918 to command 24 (Training) Wing at Grantham, and he remained in the training sphere until 1922, most of the time as Chief Flying Instructor at the new RAF College at Cranwell. Then, after attending the first RAF Staff College Course at Andover, he joined the Operations and Intelligence staff in the Air Ministry, where the quality of his work, particularly in relation to operational requirements, earned him Trenchard's high regard. There followed attendance on the Senior Officers' War Course at Greenwich, a spell in command of 7 Squadron, equipped with Vickers Virginia bombers, and in 1929 a further period of study at the Imperial Defence College. Another tour of duty in the Air Ministry came next, this time in the Plans Branch, where he was closely concerned with inter-Service matters, and in 1934 he took command of the British Forces in Aden, enabling him to gain experience of air control operations against local tribes. He was still there in 1935, as the youngest Air Commodore in the RAF, when the Italians were threatening Abyssinia and the Base had to be heavily reinforced in case of attack.

On returning home, he joined the Directing Staff at the Imperial Defence College, after which, in 1937, he became Director of Organisation in the Air Ministry. Many of the activities connected with the rapid expansion of the RAF were now his immediate concern, including sites for new airfields, the formation of new units, establishments of aircraft and personnel, and the organisational structure, and in July 1938 he was instrumental in setting up the new Maintenance Command to handle all but the higher policy aspects of maintenance and supply. Further advancement was not long delayed, for in February 1939 he joined the Air Council as Air Member for Personnel. His year in this post, covering the final peacetime months and the opening phase of the war, saw a whole series of measures that were to prove their worth in the years to come, among them the inauguration of the Empire Air Training Scheme, the creation of the Women's Auxiliary Air Force, the formation of a specialised Technical Branch, and the establishment of a Directorate of Manning. There was, moreover, no better position from which to learn about the top structure of his Service and the potentialities of its senior leaders. This knowledge would soon be put to good use, but first he needed experience of high operational command.

Portal took over Bomber Command from the senior and much respected Edgar Ludlow-Hewitt in March 1940. The bombing force that he inherited had already shown itself incapable of operating unescorted by day without prohibitive losses; and although Portal did all he could to use his aircraft both strategically and tactically during the Battle of France and to help prevent a German invasion of Great Britain, it became increasingly clear to him that for a host of technical reasons the only targets in Germany that the bombers were likely to be able to hit by night in the foreseeable future would be large industrial areas, the same sort of targets that the Luftwaffe was already attacking in the United Kingdom. Nevertheless, during his six-month stay at Bomber Command, he could do little more than try to comply with the multiplicity of Air Ministry Directives issued to him, showing what Arthur Harris, one of his Group Commanders, called a "calm confidence". As we can now see, his main achievement was to avoid unduly heavy losses and thus conserve the bomber force for the future.

That future was to be in his hands, for in October 1940 he was appointed Chief of the Air Staff. "The accepted star of the Air Force", as Churchill called him, was still only 47, much younger than his Navy and Army opposite numbers on the Chiefs of Staff Committee. Yet he could combine a highly distinguished operational record in World War I with command experience at most levels, a full sequence of staff training, and service in several key posts in the Air Ministry. That career was now to be capped by five years spent in leading his Service during the Second World War, and in playing his part in the determination of grand strategy. The range of his responsibilities was enormous, though inevitably he had to delegate much of the day-to-day work of running the Air Force to his deputies, in particular the wise and wily Sir Wilfrid Freeman, on whom he relied heavily for advice in the earlier years. It is possible here to touch on only two of the greatest RAF issues.

The first was the relation of air power to the roles of the other two Services, neither of which was initially persuaded that the RAF, strongly convinced of the importance of strategic bombing, was sufficiently concerned about its needs. Within weeks of taking office, Portal had to withstand a strong bid for the Royal Navy to take over Coastal Command, an issue which, after threatening to resign, he eventually resolved with a sensible compromise which allowed the Navy operational control. Then in 1942, General Brooke, recently appointed Chief of the Imperial General Staff, urged the formation of an Army Air Arm as the only means of providing tactical air support for the land battle, and Portal had to argue very strongly for the maintenance of the unified Air Force, pointing out that splitting up the RAF, far from increasing the number of aircraft, would merely destroy the cohesion of the nation's growing air power. Fortunately, as the war progressed and the RAF grew in strength, the complaints of the sister Services largely disappeared, and Portal deserves his full share of credit for the close co-operation and understanding that developed between the three Services at all levels from the Chiefs of Staff downwards. That the RAF played such major roles in the Battle of the Atlantic, in the Mediterranean and North West European campaigns, and in the Far Eastern war, owed much to his breadth of vision.

The second major issue was the strategic bomber offensive, a campaign in which Portal strongly believed and without whom, as Harris later concluded, it would probably never have materialised*. Convinced that it offered the one means in the early part of the war to strike directly at the enemy, but that time was needed to build up its potential, it was he that at times reinforced Churchill's determination to press on and at others allayed his doubts about what the offensive was capable of achieving. It was Portal who saw that area bombing offered the only way forward in 1942 and 1943, that Bomber Command required a new leader to inspire it, and then gave his choice, Sir Arthur Harris, the full support he needed. True, they had their differences, for example over the Pathfinder Force, the diversion of Bomber Command for Operation Overlord, and particularly the role of Bomber Command in the later stages of the war, when Portal was unable to persuade Harris of the overriding importance of the oil offensive. To say, however, as some have done, that Portal was indecisive and weak in not dismissing him over this issue, and cannot therefore be considered a great Commander, is totally unjustified. Portal realised that Harris's qualities far outweighed his defects, and bearing in mind Harris's prestige and the state of the war at that time, such a measure would have been totally inappropriate.

Reaching far beyond such essentially RAF issues were Portal's duties as a member of the Chiefs of Staff Committee. Meeting regularly, often under the Chairmanship of the Prime Minister himself, their main concerns were strategic planning and the overall direction of military operations, and here he more than held his own, not only with his older colleagues, but also with Churchill, to whom he would always stand up when necessary, and with whom he had considerable influence. Indeed, Lord Ismay, who was Churchill's Military Representative on the Committee, and thus the best placed observer, saw Portal as quite easily the greatest British Commander during the war, a view which also took account of his role in the even wider dimension of Anglo-American relations.

Even before the United States entered the war, Portal had met General Arnold and other leaders of the United States Army Air Corps and had earned their confidence. His subsequent total support for the USAAF build-up in the United Kingdom, his backing of their daylight bombing policy which he realised would complement the RAF's night offensive, and his encouragement when things were going wrong, won him the unstinted admiration and respect

* See page 29

of all the American airmen who knew him. Indeed, on occasions, it was his advocacy rather than General Arnold's that won the day in top debate about the mission of the Eighth Air Force. He earned similar high regard for his contribution to the Combined Chiefs of Staff; when accompanying Churchill and his other British colleagues to most of the great Allied planning conferences, it was often – as Eisenhower and others later testified – his quiet, dispassionate reasoning that would reconcile the differences and produce the mutually acceptable formula for agreement. This success with the Americans in what was essentially a coalition war was seen by Maurice Dean as one of Portal's greatest achievements.

As the conflict drew to an end in 1945, the longest serving of the Chiefs of Staff was still aged only 52, and while the accolades poured in, amid the succession of victory celebrations, Portal was preparing to hand over the reins. Many issues, however, still engaged his attention in the closing months of 1945, including the building up of Transport Command, the start of demobilisation, and in particular the far-reaching consequences of the invention of the atomic bomb. Indeed, the concept of the strategic nuclear deterrent was already formulated before he left office at the end of December, and his experience and understanding of the great issues made the now Lord Portal the obvious choice of the Prime Minister, Clement Attlee, to head the new Atomic Energy organisation. By the time he retired, almost six years later, the explosion of Britain's first atomic bomb was only a year away, and despite the lack of help from the USA, the shortage of money, and constraints of security, great progress had been made in developing the new technology for civil as well as military purposes. Though a somewhat reluctant Controller, his prestige and ability at the political level were essential to the progress of the programme in those early days.

From 1952 onwards, it was the business world that claimed much of his attention, and particularly the British Aircraft Corporation of which he became the Chairman in 1960. Issues such as the cancellation of the TSR2, which he fought hard to preserve, and the development of the Concorde ensured that he remained fully occupied, and it was only in 1969 that he finally retired. Throughout these post-war years, while never seeking to influence his successors on matters of RAF policy, he had retained his Service contacts, and two organisations, the RAF Benevolent Fund and the RAF Escaping Society, were particularly close to his heart.

He died in 1971, and four years later the statue that commemorates him in Whitehall Gardens was unveiled by Mr Harold Macmillan. Significantly, it stands not far from that of Trenchard, symbolising the relationship between the young Service's two greatest leaders.

Portal was a man who took some knowing, often appearing cold, remote and enigmatic as John Terraine describes him. Those close to him, however, often saw the kind and human side, and all understood the pressure under which he laboured as CAS for most of the war. To R V Jones, who often had to advise him on scientific matters, he was highly supportive and had tremendous authority; to Slessor, he was wise and very patient; to Maurice Dean, he was the complete professional; to Tedder, he was the real brains in the Chiefs of Staff; to Mountbatten, he was a great co-operator; to Eisenhower, he was a man who enjoyed great prestige, with the Americans as well as the British. Let Churchill have the last word: "Portal had everything."

Marshal of the Royal Air Force
Sir Arthur Harris

Of all the high commanders of the Royal Air Force during the Second World War, the most widely known is probably Sir Arthur Harris. Yet the mere mention of his name still arouses the deepest passions and arguments, for the strategic bombing offensive which he so ably led has caused more controversy than any other campaign that was waged against Germany. Inevitably therefore, his reputation and his place in history depend heavily on how one assesses the role and achievements of Bomber Command under his direction.

Arthur Harris was born in Cheltenham in 1892. Sixteen years later, seeking adventure, he went to Rhodesia and worked in a variety of jobs – mining, farming, coach driving among them – until the outbreak of war in 1914 when he joined the 1st Rhodesia Regiment as a bugler and took part in the short campaign in German South West Africa. Then, anxious for closer involvement in the wartime action, he returned to England, was accepted for the Royal Flying Corps and completed his pilot training in January 1916. He first flew operationally with 39 Squadron against the Zeppelins; then after a period with day fighters in France he returned to England to train a new night fighter squadron at Marham, and later in 1918 took command of 44 Squadron on the Western Front. Hardly had the war ended than, to his surprise, he was offered a permanent commission.

1919 and 1920 were unsatisfactory years, spent largely in closing down unwanted units, and in his first overseas command, of 31 Squadron at Cawnpore in 1921, he was strongly critical of the poor administrative support provided him by the Army and considered resignation. A switch to Iraq to take over 45 Squadron proved more to his liking; in the air control operations then underway he made imaginative use of the Vickers Vernon for bombing as well as its normal role of troop-carrying. His next tour was in command of 58 Squadron based at Worthy Down and equipped with Virginias, the heavy bombers of the day, and there followed two years as a student at the Army Staff College Camberley, a spell as Senior Staff Officer to the AOC Middle East Command, and several months as OC 210 (Flying Boat) Squadron at Pembroke Dock. Here, as during his time with 58 Squadron, he laid much stress on the importance of operating by night. Thus by 1933 he had acquired wide experience of many types of flying, much of it as a squadron commander, and was a trained and practised staff officer with considerable knowledge of the other Services.

So far, however, he had no direct experience of the Air Ministry, a shortcoming now to be remedied by a brief spell as Deputy Director of Operations and Intelligence followed by three years as Deputy Director of Plans. Here he was involved in many of the policy issues of the mid-1930s, including projects for new types of aircraft, and as the RAF member of the

Chiefs of Staff Joint Planning Committee he helped draw up the various war plans. The joint appreciation of the situation in the event of war with Germany which he and his Navy and Army colleagues prepared was shown by later events to have been remarkably perceptive.

There followed from 1937 onwards a series of frequent postings. He served for a year as AOC 4 Group, which was then re-equipping with the Whitley; he spent a month in the USA on an aircraft purchasing mission; reluctant to go to Fighter Command as SASO in 1938 he went instead as AOC to Palestine, where the RAF and Army were increasingly committed to helping the civil authorities in the face of Arab/Jewish hostilities; and on the outbreak of war he returned to Bomber Command, this time as AOC 5 Group, which operated the Hampdens. Here he remained until November 1940, working hard to rectify the many deficiencies of the force he led to ensure that it played whatever part it could in the difficult early days of the war. He devoted much effort to improving training, not least by forming an Operational Training Unit of the type that would later be so essential to the functioning of Bomber Command as a whole, and while his Hampdens were used on bombing operations whenever possible, Harris soon perceived that their most valuable role was minelaying. However, as he knew only too well, there was still much to be done before Bomber Command could contribute with real effect, and when Portal brought him back to the Air Ministry in November 1940 as Deputy Chief of Air Staff it was so that he could oversee the build-up of the RAF – and not least of Bomber Command. Thus it was that Harris witnessed at first hand the worst of the German bombing of London. A mere six months later he was on the move again, this time to head the RAF Delegation in Washington at a time when United States aid was becoming of overriding importance and closer ties were being developed with the US Army Air Corps. Now only one further posting lay ahead. It came in February 1942 when he was selected to become Commander-in-Chief of Bomber Command, the post for which he was ideally suited both by experience and by inclination.

The policy he was to implement for the rest of the war had in effect been determined in 1940 when Great Britain and her Commonwealth partners stood alone after the fall of France. The options then had been starkly simple: come to terms with Hitler, or wage a largely defensive war against the hope that circumstances might eventually change, or take the offensive in the only way then possible – by strategic bombing. Inevitably, however, in view of the shortcomings of the bomber force then in existence, it would take time before the campaign could have significant effect, and by early 1942 it seemed to the many critics that the offensive was achieving little in relation to the enormous efforts being devoted to it. Yet to abandon it would have meant a fundamental change of strategy which would have wasted much of the work of the preceding years, removed the only means of bringing active support to the Soviet Union, and probably persuaded the USA to concentrate its main effort against Japan rather than Germany. The strongest of arguments thus existed for pressing on with the bomber offensive in 1942; what was needed was the man to lead and inspire it.

Harris rose superbly to the challenge. Very quickly, by the force of his personality and convictions, he gave his men confidence in themselves, in the importance of the job they were doing, and in their leadership – and he did it

18 *Sir Hugh Dowding accompanying the King and Queen during a visit to Bentley Priory, September 1940.*

19 *Lord Dowding with a group of his Battle of Britain pilots at a reunion. Left to right: Sqn Ldr A C Bartley, Wg Cdr D F B Sheen, Wg Cdr I R Gleed, Wg Cdr M Aitken, Wg Cdr A G Malan, Sqn Ldr A C Deere, Lord Dowding, Flt Off E C Henderson, Flt Lt R H Hillary, Wg Cdr J A Kent, Wg Cdr C B F Kingcome, Sqn Ldr D H Watkins, W/O R H Gretton.*

20 *Lord Dowding laying the Foundation Stone of the Battle of Britain Memorial Chapel at Biggin Hill, 24 July 1951. In attendance is Air Vice-Marshal The Earl of Bandon.*

21 *Lord Dowding unveils a stone plaque above the site of the 11 Group underground Operations Room at RAF Uxbridge, 22 April 1958. With him is Air Vice Marshal V S Bowling AOC 11 Group.*

22 In 1917 Field Marshal Smuts took a prominent part in the War Cabinet deliberations which led to the formation of the Royal Air Force. Twenty-five years later, in November 1942, he was in London and a commemorative photograph was taken with the Air Council and the Air Officers Commanding-in-Chief of most of the Home Commands. Left to right – seated: Air Chief Marshal Sir Philip Joubert (AOCinC Coastal Command), Lord Sherwood (Parliamentary Under-Secretary), Captain J D Smuts, Air Chief Marshal Sir Charles Portal (CAS), Field Marshal The Rt Hon J C Smuts, The Rt Hon Sir Archibald Sinclair (Secretary of State for Air), Mr S F Waterson (High Commissioner for South Africa), Captain The Rt Hon H H Balfour (Parliamentary Under-Secretary), Air Chief Marshal Sir Christopher Courtney (AMSO), Air Chief Marshal Sir Sholto Douglas (AOCinC Fighter Command). Left to right – standing: Air Marshal A G R Garrod (Air Member for Training), Air Marshal Sir John Babington (AOCinC Technical Training Command), Sir Harold Howitt, Air Marshal F J Linnell (Controller of Research and Development, MAP), Air Chief Marshal Sir Edgar Ludlow-Hewitt (Inspector-General), Sir Arthur Street (PUS), Air Marshal P Babington (AOCinC Flying Training Command), Air Marshal D G Donald (AOCinC Maintenance Command), Air Marshal Sir Bertine Sutton (AMP), Air Marshal Sir Arthur Barratt (AOCinC Army Co-operation Command), Air Marshal Sir Leslie Gossage (AOCinC Balloon Command), Air Marshal C E H Medhurst (temporary VCAS).

23 *Sir Charles Portal accompanies the King,*
25 June 1943.

24 *Sir Charles Portal with the Prime Minister,*
returning from an overseas visit.

25 *Sir Charles Portal,*
accompanied by Air Vice-
Marshal Park, talks to fighter
pilots in Malta,
8 February 1943.

26 *Sir Charles Portal in*
discussion with Air Vice-
Marshal Dickson, AOC Desert
Air Force, in Italy: 28 August
1944.

27 Squadron Leader Harris, OC 45 Squadron in Iraq in 1922, with the squadron football team.

28 Sir Arthur Harris attends a conference of the Allied Expeditionary Air Force in August 1944.
Seated at the table (from left to right) are Lieutenant Colonel D Heathcote-Amery (21st Army
Group), Major General R Royce (Deputy Air CinC, AEAF), Air Chief Marshal Sir Sholto
Douglas (AOCinC Coastal Command), Air Chief Marshal Sir Arthur Harris (AOCinC Bomber
Command), Air Chief Marshal Sir Trafford Leigh-Mallory (Air CinC, AEAF), Major General F L
Anderson (US Strategic Air Forces), Lieutenant General J H Doolittle (Commanding General 8th
Air Force), Brigadier General F L Parks (US Strategic Air Forces), Air Marshal Sir Roderic Hill
(ADGB).

29 Sir Arthur Harris and Lady Harris (on the right), pay a return visit to High Wycombe, now Headquarters Strike Command, on 3 June 1972. They are welcomed by the AOCinC, Sir Andrew Humphrey, and Lady Humphrey.

30 Sir Arthur Harris visiting one of his old stations, RAF Wyton, on 28 June 1957.

31 *Sir Sholto Douglas, in the company of Mr Churchill and General Sir Alan Brooke, Chief of the Imperial General Staff, admiring the dachshund belonging to Lady Casey, wife of the Minister of State in Cairo, in February 1943.*

32 *Air Vice-Marshal Douglas, AOC 11 Group, decorates a Polish Flight Lieutenant, December 1940.*

33 *Sir Sholto Douglas, as AOCinC Middle East.*

despite very rarely visiting an operational station. Moreover he quickly demonstrated to Churchill and his colleagues that Bomber Command might well, given the strength, actually be able to do what its proponents had always claimed; certainly from now on all knew that the war could and would be taken to the enemy homeland on an ever-increasing scale. The means of doing so were largely by area bombing, a policy since strongly criticised in many quarters but in practice the only one the RAF could effectively follow up to 1944 owing to the inability of the bomber to survive over Germany by day and to find and hit precision targets by night. This policy, clearly laid down by the War Cabinet and Chiefs of Staff, was fully in line with Harris's own views, and for two years he did everything in his power to build up the strength of his command and improve its techniques and tactics in order to implement it. The thousand bomber raids of 1942, the Battles of the Ruhr and Hamburg in 1943, the Battle of Berlin in 1943/44: these were but landmarks in a steadily mounting campaign that caused enormous damage to many of the cities and industries of Germany and forced the enemy to devote increasing resources to home defence and damage repair.

The strategic bomber offensive became, of course, over these years very much a joint operation with the United States 8th Army Air Force, and throughout Harris gave his American colleagues every encouragement and assistance. Quick to see the advantages of being able to attack Germany by day as well as night, Harris never allowed his doubts about their proposed tactics to affect the backing he gave them, and the generous tributes he himself paid them afterwards were amply reflected in those he received in return. The alliance between the two air forces which Harris did so much to forge and has remained so important in the post-war years must count as one of his greatest achievements.

The area offensive against Germany was not, however, the only task laid upon Harris and his men; indeed what he usually described as 'diversions' required a very substantial share of their efforts at various stages of the war. His reluctance to attack what he called panacea targets, or to support the Battle of the Atlantic by attacking submarine bases in France rather than their production facilities in Germany, for example, was made abundantly clear to those in higher authority. Then in 1944 when it was decided to place the strategic air forces at the disposal of General Eisenhower for Operation Overlord, he protested in the strongest terms at what he saw as the abandonment of the offensive against Germany, which he firmly believed could force her surrender on its own if properly applied. Yet if Harris was always ready to argue his case, he was also fully prepared to do what he was told when the decision went against him, and in the event he gave to the Normandy invasion campaign his unstinted support; as Eisenhower told General Marshall in September 1944, "Harris actually proved to be one of the most effective and co-operative members of my team; he met every request."

Had the war finished at this point, the verdict on Harris and the bomber offensive might well have proved much less equivocal than it has generally been. Sadly, however, the pattern of the strategic campaign in the closing months of the war has tended to cast a shadow over its total achievement, and when one considers the immense hitting power now available and the general weakness of the German defences it is hard not to believe that more emphasis could – and should – have been placed upon attacking carefully selected precision targets rather than on the continued bombing of centres of population. But in saying that one must remember the remarkable resilience still being shown by the Germans, demonstrated not least in the Ardennes offensive, the V1 and V2 weapon campaigns, and their new technological developments. For the leaders of the time what really mattered was to use all means to bring the war to an end as quickly as possible, and Harris and his men played their full part.

For them, however, victory had a hollow ring. Churchill made no reference to them in his broadcast on VE day; there was no award of a special medal for the men of Bomber Command; nor did Harris himself receive the peerage with which the other great Service commanders were honoured – though he was promoted to Marshal of the Royal Air Force, the highest recognition his own Service could bestow. To all too many it seemed that the Government and nation, having realised the destruction wrought by Bomber Command, wished to distance themselves from it. For Harris, who was utterly convinced of the essential contribution of his men to the Allied victory and well aware of the cost of their achievement in human terms, this was shameful treatment and he never forgot it, though he did appreciate Churchill's offer to make amends to him personally in 1953, when he was offered a peerage and accepted a baronetcy.

When the war ended he was aged 53. Unless he were to become Chief of the Air Staff or perhaps Inspector General, there was no further RAF post open to him, and rather than enter public life in the United Kingdom he resolved to retire to South Africa. Some of his American friends, however, had other ideas and in 1946 he agreed to become Managing Director of a new shipping line, the South African Marine Corporation, operating between the USA and South Africa. This work was to keep him occupied for many years, and he remained aloof from the continuing controversies surrounding Bomber Command. But as the years moved on and he outlived so many of his contemporaries, he felt again his responsibility to try to ensure that the men he had led were properly commemorated and their reputations protected. He always gave full support to the Bomber Command Association, and the Aircrew Association – founded in 1977 – owed much to his inspiration, as its first President; his address to them at Guildhall on his 90th birthday showed that he had lost none of his fire and wit. The Bomber Command Museum too, whose opening he attended on 12 April 1983, he saw as a fitting memorial. He died a year later, aged almost 92, the last of the RAF's great captains and certainly its greatest operational commander in the Second World War.

About a commander such as Harris, single-minded, utterly determined, convinced of the rightness of his own opinions, there are bound to be different views. But surely none would dispute his quality as a leader, as a man prepared to take responsibility and make decisions. As Maurice Dean reminds us, for over three years he had to put the lives of his squadrons and the future of his Command at risk many times each month; such continuous strain has few parallels in history. The real questions surround the value of the operations which he directed and here – as one looks back with the perspectives of history – there is no doubt that they played a crucial part in the defeat of Hitler's Germany.

Marshal of the Royal Air Force
The Lord Douglas

Lord Douglas shares with Sir Arthur Harris the signal distinction of being promoted to the most senior rank in the Royal Air Force without having filled the post of Chief of the Air Staff. To have been so recognised was clearly the reflection of the qualities he had displayed in four successive appointments as a Commander-in-Chief over a five-year span from late 1940 until the end of 1945: none of his contemporaries could equal his sustained and widely varied experience of top operational command.

Born in 1893, Sholto Douglas went from Tonbridge School to Oxford in 1913 to read 'Greats' but when the war interrupted his studies a year later he was commissioned in the Royal Horse Artillery and went to France. In early 1915 his interest in flying, which had been first aroused while still a schoolboy, led him to volunteer for observer duties with the Royal Flying Corps and on joining 2 Squadron at Merville his first flight was on an operational mission. Soon afterwards he was accepted for pilot training and within three months he was back in France flying with 8 Squadron and heavily engaged in the air fighting during the earlier phase of the Fokker scourge. Most of 1916 he spent in supervising flying training at Montrose and forming the new 43 Squadron before taking it to France in January 1917. Four months and much heavy fighting later, he was injured when his aircraft crashed on take-off, but by September he was fit enough to return to operations, this time in command of 84 Squadron which he led for the rest of the war, gaining further experience in the use of fighters both in air combat and in ground support.

Obviously well thought of, a permanent career in the post-war RAF was his for the asking, but his own inclinations lay towards what he saw as the greater challenge of civil aviation and he joined Handley Page's Air Transport Company. Yet despite the fascination of flying the large HP 0/400 and V/1500 he remained uncertain about his future and a chance meeting with Trenchard in 1920 led to his rejoining the RAF. His first appointment was to a staff post at 1 Group, Kenley, after which he became Chief Flying Instructor at 6 Flying Training School, Manston and then attended the first Staff College Course at Andover. There followed an Air Ministry appointment concerned with flying training from 1923 to 1926, attendance at the Imperial Defence College, and then command of the RAF station at North Weald, from where in 1929 he made the last of his several appearances in the Hendon Air Display. Next came a spell as senior RAF officer in the Sudan and a long tour as RAF Instructor at the Imperial Defence College, where he had dealings with many officers whom he would subsequently work with during the war.

Thus, by 1936 he had combined extensive flying experience, mainly in the fighter role, with staff work at various levels and much opportunity to study and think about air power and strategy, and after a short period attending the

Italian Army manoeuvres he began a spell of duty in the Air Ministry that was to last five years, covering the main RAF expansion period and the opening phases of the war. To begin with, as Director of Staff Duties, his concerns were with operational and staff officer training; and in 1938, as Assistant Chief of Air Staff, his responsibilities were extended to cover operational requirements. Thus new types of aircraft and equipment were now within his bailiwick, and among other things he devoted much effort to the development of radar. Two years later, in 1940, he joined the Air Council as Deputy Chief of Air Staff, responsible for all current RAF operations, and throughout the disasters in Scandinavia, the Low Countries and France and the subsequent testing time of the Battle of Britain he was at the heart of the RAF's affairs, maintaining close contact with the Commands and often deputising for CAS on major issues. It was hardly surprising, therefore, that when it was decided to relieve Dowding at Fighter Command Douglas should be chosen to succeed him.

The immediate challenge facing him was to counter the Luftwaffe's growing night bombing campaign against the United Kingdom; while Fighter Command had established superiority by day during the Battle of Britain, it was still very far from being able to intercept night bombers on any scale. The obvious solution seemed to lie in the work already being carried out on airborne radar, but much still remained to be done to enable this research to be applied, and it was not until well into 1941 that Douglas's night fighters began to achieve real success. From then on, however, the Luftwaffe would never be able to attack the United Kingdom by day or night without incurring heavy losses. At the same time Douglas was eager to take the war to the enemy, and the offensive patrols which his fighters began to undertake over North East France in early 1941 became of particular importance when the Germans attacked the Soviet Union and it was necessary to try to compel the Luftwaffe to maintain its strength in the West. This role was extended in 1942 when the fighters began to escort the light bombers in sweeps across the Channel, known as Circus operations, and in August Douglas, who was now air representative on the joint Anglo-American Committee that was beginning to plan for the eventual invasion of North West Europe, directed his fighters during the Dieppe Raid, when the Luftwaffe was kept away from the area and much was learnt about the methods of air support for a seaborne landing.

It was with understandable disappointment that Douglas now heard that he was to move to Cairo to take over Middle East Command from Tedder. While there had been great operational activity over the previous two years, by the time Douglas arrived at the end of 1942 the main battles were about to move away to the central Mediterranean, and although he had responsibilities extending as far as Iran, Aden, Sudan and East Africa, the principal theatre of operations was outside his concern. Diplomatic commitments, both in Egypt itself and in other countries such as Turkey, took some of his time; he did much to assist the build-up of the USAAF in the Eastern Mediterranean; he was in charge of a major air transport force and a great spread of staging posts; and in autumn 1943 he was closely involved in the Dodecanese operations which were intended to exploit the Italian surrender and bring the Turks into the war. This was an unhappy episode in which Douglas felt he had been given inadequate resources for the job required of him, and it was with relief that he heard at the end of the year of plans to move him yet again. Suggestions that he should become Supreme Commander of the new South East Asia Command and later that he should serve as deputy to General Eaker in Italy having come to naught, he was now chosen to go to Northwood to take over Coastal Command from John Slessor. Writing to Churchill at that time, Sir Archibald Sinclair said: "I entirely agree with your estimate of Douglas; there is no appointment in the RAF for which I should not be glad to recommend him."

Though maritime operations had hitherto been largely outside his experience, this was a post much more to Douglas's liking, not least because it would place him close to the centre of the action for the remainder of the war. Coastal Command was by early 1944 a formidable organisation, working in close co-operation with the Royal Navy and with responsibilities extending from Iceland to Gibraltar and far out into the Atlantic. Ever since the beginning of the war it had been engaged in the great campaign to defeat the German U-boat offensive, and although the turning point had been reached in 1943 there could be no respite in the maritime patrol and convoy escort operations so essential to protect the North Atlantic supply route. Coastal Command was also responsible for the unspectacular but indispensable work of the meteorological squadrons as well as for the Photographic Reconnaisance Unit, and it was increasingly engaged in offensive operations through the activities of its Strike Wings against German shipping. There was thus much activity to occupy the attention of the Commander-in-Chief, but Douglas was at the same time closely involved in the planning and preparations for the Normandy invasion. While – unlike the other United Kingdom Air Forces – his Command did not come under the control of the Allied Supreme Commander, it would have much to do in patrolling the approaches to the Channel area and protecting the invasion forces from German surface and submarine attack. In the event the invasion fleets and the subsequent cross-Channel supply routes were kept almost totally free from enemy interference, an achievement for which Coastal Command and the Royal Navy must share the credit.

During the closing phases of the war the pattern of the anti-submarine war changed, since French bases were no longer available to the U-boats, but the Germans were still not beaten and their development of new tactics largely connected with the introduction of the schnorkel presented Douglas and his men with a further disturbing challenge. At the same time he steadily extended the operations of his Strike Wings against enemy shipping along the coasts of Northern Europe, contributing much to the eventual German collapse though not without substantial losses. For Coastal Command, larger with its force of 800 aircraft than at any other time in its history, there could be no relaxation until all fighting ceased.

With the end of the war came the tributes, none more appreciated than that from Portal: "No-one in the whole of the RAF has given in fuller measure, personally or officially, the support and loyal co-operation without which I could not have carried on . . . you have done magnificently every job entrusted to you." But more jobs lay ahead, and clearly one possibility was that, at the age of 52, he would succeed Portal as Chief of the Air Staff. This was not to be: instead he was to spend his final years in the RAF in Germany. He went there initially – and reluctantly – as Commander of the British Air Forces of Occupation, where he answered to Field Marshal Montgomery, the Military Governor of the British Zone. His task of controlling the Tactical Air Force was relatively simple; far more difficult were the problems of disarming the Luftwaffe amidst a devastated Germany, the question of access to the Western Sectors of Berlin, and such political issues as the return home of Czech and Polish airmen who had been serving with the RAF. Matters of this kind were not to the taste of one who preferred operational command and in January 1946 he decided to retire.

Yet if he did not enjoy such work he had obviously done it to the general satisfaction, for he was unanimously chosen by the Cabinet of Clement Attlee to take over from Montgomery. So on 1 May 1946, though far from enthusiastic about his new role, he became Commander-in-Chief of the Armed Forces and Military Governor of the British Zone of Germany and British Member of the Four-Power Allied Control Council in Berlin. For a Royal Air Force officer this was a unique appointment, and he held it during a critical period when the strains between the Soviet Union and the Western Allies in occupied Germany were becoming acute. On the one hand the Russians were demanding enormous reparations and trying to remove every item that might be useful to them; on the other the Allies realised that the burden of feeding and administering a ruined Germany was impossible unless the Germans themselves were allowed to play a proper role. The decision to fuse the British and American Zones economically in July 1946 was the first major step along the road to the East-West division that was to mark Germany for more than 40 years, but the problems continued, exacerbated by the exceptionally harsh winter of 1946/47, and Douglas increasingly felt that the situation required political rather than military skills.

To his great distress, he also had to act as British member of the final Court of Appeal against the sentences passed on the German war criminals at the Nuremberg Tribunal. This entailed much study of the relevant documents, lengthy procedural discussions, and a great deal of personal heart-searching, for he had his doubts about the legality of the trials and was not happy about the British Government's attempts to pressurise him. In the event he went along with his Soviet, American and French colleagues in confirming the sentences but desperately wished he had never needed to be involved.

For Douglas this had been the unhappiest period in his entire official life, and he was eventually released from his duties in Germany in November 1947. His services in both the military and political fields were now recognised by the award of a peerage, and he took his seat on the Labour benches in the House of Lords. Soon afterwards he joined the Board of the British Overseas Airways Corporation and then, in early 1949, accepted the Government's invitation to become Chairman of British European Airways. He held this position for 15 years, seeing the airline through a period of great development and expansion into the jet era. On retirement in 1964 he became Chairman of Horizon Travel but soon his health began to fail and he died in 1969.

Certainly Lord Douglas was among the greatest wartime leaders of the RAF, though through no fault of his own he had the habit, as John Terraine remarks, of arriving in his chief appointments too late for the great days. The Battle of Britain was won before he reached Fighter Command, El Alamein was over just prior to his arrival in the Middle East, the crisis point in the Battle of the Atlantic was past when he reached Coastal Command, and the war was won when he went to Germany. Yet in a sense these unlucky timings made the challenges facing him all the greater, and the decision to select him for his final appointment in Germany must be a measure of his stature as a leader. As Maurice Dean describes him he was "the complete professional. Shrewd, capable, tough, experienced, intelligent, he served the RAF well."

Marshal of the Royal Air Force
The Lord Tedder

That Lord Tedder is remembered mainly for his role in securing the Allied victory in the West is probably not surprising, but what is less often recalled is that he was also one of the longer serving Chiefs of the Air Staff. Older than Portal, whom he succeeded, he led the Royal Air Force through the first four very difficult post-war years, and he remained in harness – representing his country in the USA – even longer. By 1951, when he departed the official scene, the main post-war pattern of international relationships was firmly established and the RAF well set upon its modern course.

Arthur Tedder was born in 1890, and having read History at Magdalene College, Cambridge from 1909-1913 was in Fiji embarking on a career in the Colonial Service when war broke out. Determined to play his part he returned home and was commissioned in the Dorset Regiment. Then, after a leg injury suffered during training had barred him from the infantry, he spent a whole year persuading bureaucracy to let him join the Royal Flying Corps. 1916 saw him undergoing ground training at Reading, pilot training at Thetford, and joining 25 Squadron in France in time to fly operationally during the Battle of the Somme. The qualities he then demonstrated led to Trenchard choosing him to command 70 Squadron in early 1917, and in June he returned home to command 67 Training Squadron at Shawbury. A year later, his ship having been torpedoed en route, he was in Egypt running 38 Training Wing.

With the war over, and firmly decided to stay in the RAF rather than rejoin the Colonial Service, Tedder was given command of 274 (later 207) Squadron, and in 1921 he took 207 to Turkey as part of the British Expeditionary Force deployed during the Chanak Incident. There followed, after he had completed the course at the Naval Staff College, the first of a series of postings that capitalised on his wartime experience of training and would make him one of the leading experts in this sphere. From 1924 to 1926 he commanded 2 Flying Training School at Digby, where he insisted on the highest standards and was alerted to some of the basic deficiencies of the RAF's flying training system; 1927 he spent in the Directorate of Training in the Air Ministry; from 1929 to 1931, having passed the previous year at the Imperial Defence College, he was on the Directing Staff of the RAF Staff College Andover; and between 1932 and 1934 he was CO of the Air Armament School at Eastchurch, where he did much to make the training more practical and realistic. Hardly surprisingly he was then selected to become Director of Training, where he did his utmost – against severe financial constraints – to introduce new ideas. The need to exploit the potential of civilian flying schools, with the Central Flying School ensuring proper standards, he saw as particularly important and the later vast expansion of flying training owed much to his efforts in these relatively early days.

In October 1936 came a complete change of scene when he went to

Singapore as AOC Far East Air Force. By now so-called 'Fortress Singapore' was well on its way to completion, and Tedder's main concerns – apart from local politics – were to develop the RAF's new landing grounds in Malaya and improve its standards of training. Like many others on the spot, however, he had few illusions about the adequacy of the local defences and he was fortunate to return home well before the outbreak of hostilities. His new task was to take charge of research and development under Sir Wilfrid Freeman, and from July 1938 he was closely concerned in the planning and production of new types of aircraft equipment. He thus had a key role in the critical months before and after the beginning of the war, and when he joined Beaverbrook's Ministry of Aircraft Production in the summer of 1940 he seemed destined to remain behind the scenes. Portal, however, had other ideas and well aware that Tedder was not enamoured of Beaverbrook proposed him as Deputy Commander in Chief in the increasingly important Middle East theatre. Churchill refused to agree, for Tedder did not impress him, but when Air Vice Marshal Boyd was taken prisoner after force-landing in Sicily on his way to take over in Cairo, Portal was able to persuade the Prime Minister that Tedder must be appointed.

During the next three years Tedder was to imprint himself on the history of the air war in the Mediterranean, first as Deputy to Sir Arthur Longmore at Middle East Command, then as his successor there, and finally as Air Commander-in-Chief for the whole Mediterranean theatre. He faced many problems in the first two years: shortage of aircraft of the right types, major difficulties in supply and maintenance, conflicting pressures for his scarce resources to be deployed to meet emergency situations such as those in Greece, Syria, Iraq and not least the Far East. He also had to contend with much sniping at home, including on one occasion a major attempt to have him replaced. These were indeed difficult years, marked not least by the loss of Crete, the long drawn-out conflict over and around Malta, and the series of desert battles against Rommel that switched repeatedly between success and defeat, and there were many in the other Services who were all too ready to blame their difficulties upon the lack of proper air support. It is the measure of Tedder's achievement that by the time of the Battle of El Alamein most of the critics had been silenced. His insistence, and that of his immediate subordinates such as 'Mary' Coningham, that the winning of the air battle must take precedence, and that the whole air, sea and land campaign must be run as a fully combined operation, was fundamental to the desert victory. Thus was sown, and not least through his own rapport with General Auchinleck, the close cooperation between the air and land forces that was to be the key to the great Allied victories which lay ahead in the Central Mediterranean and North West Europe.

By the end of 1942 Tedder was held in high regard, and not just for his share in the defeat of Rommel at El Alamein. He had acquired Churchill's confidence to the extent of accompanying him to Moscow in the previous August, he was delighted that the newly arrived General Montgomery had set cooperation with the RAF as his first priority, and he was showing himself adept at getting on with the leaders of the steadily increasing number of United States Army Air Force units that were arriving in the Middle Eastern theatre to operate alongside the RAF. To Portal he now seemed the right man to succeed

Freeman as Vice Chief of the Air Staff, but hardly had the necessary moves been set in train than the Allied leaders meeting at Casablanca decided to pursue a Mediterranean strategy during 1943, to appoint General Eisenhower as the Allied Theatre Commander, and to create an Air Commander-in-Chief who would control on his behalf all the Allied Air Forces. For this post Tedder was the automatic choice.

Thus throughout 1943 Tedder worked with Eisenhower, first during the Tunisian battles, next in the planning for and conduct of the Sicilian invasion, and then during the earlier stages of the long Italian campaign. Under his command was a complete air force covering every major role of air power and drawn from many nations, and Tedder showed great skill in welding together its various elements, exploiting their flexibility, and helping ensure that air, sea and land could work in harmony. Inevitably there were differences, not least with Montgomery over such matters as the need for the early capture of Sicilian airfields, and he had to argue firmly with Portal in order to retain his full air strength for the Italian landings, but Eisenhower had the highest opinion of Tedder whose technique of persuasive leadership was eminently suited to the task.

There was consequently little doubt that, when Eisenhower was chosen as Supreme Allied Commander for Operation Overlord and needed a leading British 'coalition general' as his deputy, the choice would fall upon Tedder. His appointment had the added merit that he could also direct all the air forces that were to be placed under Eisenhower's command, strategic as well as tactical. So from the beginning of 1944 Tedder played the key role in the preparation of the air campaign for Overlord, and the transportation plan by which the air forces would aim to cut all the German communications into the invasion area owed much to his advocacy. He had already experimented with this strategy in Italy and his conviction that the bombing would be accurate enough to avoid heavy casualties amongst the French civilians not only overcame the doubters but was in the event fully justified. Just as important to the success of Overlord were the many other types of air operation that were designed to win air supremacy and then support the invasion forces in all possible ways, and until the end of the war Tedder retained responsibility for coordinating the Allied air operations. As Eisenhower's deputy he was also caught up in the various disputes that arose concerning the conduct of the campaign as a whole: he was frequently critical of Montgomery's methods of conducting the battle, and appreciating better than many the importance of avoiding Anglo-American dissension he gave Eisenhower his unstinted support. Not surprisingly it was Tedder whom Eisenhower sent to Moscow in January 1945 to ascertain Soviet intentions during the closing stages of the war, and it was he who led the Western delegation to Berlin in May to sign with the Russians the ratification of the German surrender.

Now aged 55 and shortly to be promoted to Marshal of the Royal Air Force and raised to the peerage, Tedder was now recognised internationally as one of his country's most distinguished wartime leaders; not only had he proved himself a brilliant exponent of air power but he had also been one of the greatest British cooperators within the Anglo-American alliance. There now lay ahead a new challenge, for in January 1946 he succeeded Portal as Chief of the Air Staff. His task was daunting. On the one hand the RAF still had inescapable responsibilities extending across the world from Germany to the Mediterranean, the Middle East, India, Singapore and Hong Kong. On the other hand most of its skilled and experienced personnel were anxious to return to civilian life, its aircraft were largely obsolescent, and financial pressures were becoming acute.

Understandably, therefore, some of Tedder's biggest problems during his four years as CAS were on the manpower front; indeed in 1948 he warned that manning levels might in time dictate the order of battle, and he aroused the ire of the Secretary of State by not consulting him before making a widely reported speech at Halton that urged the necessity of increased recruiting. Fortunately the introduction of the peacetime National Service scheme in 1949 did much to alleviate the situation. Many measures were also taken to improve the organisation of the Service during these years, not least the introduction of several new officer branches and the development of a new trade structure. At the same time much was done to enhance the RAF's operational capability; major aircraft projects included those for the Canberra and the V Force, and the decisions in 1948 to restore the UK radar, control and reporting system and in 1949 to double the size of Fighter Command were also of great significance.

Much of Tedder's work, however, was as Chairman of the Chiefs of Staff Committee, a role to which he was well suited except when it came to dealing with Montgomery, his Army colleague, who was temperamentally unsuited to committee work and had been highly critical of Tedder as Deputy Supreme Commander. Consequently the Chiefs of Staff did not work together as well as they should have done during the immediate post-war years when faced by so many far-reaching issues. In the Far East there was continued strife in the Dutch East Indies; great problems arose from the decisions to grant independence to India and then agree to partition; and 1948 saw the outbreak of the communist insurrection in Malaya. In the Middle East there were the events associated with the relinquishment of the Palestine mandate. In Europe there were the increasing Soviet domination of Eastern Europe, culminating in the Berlin Blockade, and the many negotiations that eventually led to the signature of the North Atlantic Treaty in 1949. In these and many more issues Tedder was heavily involved, and he showed particularly close interest both in the RAF's contribution to the Berlin Airlift and in the deployment of USAF strategic bombers to Europe and the allocation of RAF airfields for their use.

Although Tedder handed over the duties of CAS at the end of 1949 there remained one more official task. The close ties with the American military leaders which he had built up during the war and continued to maintain as CAS made him the ideal choice to go to Washington as Chairman of the Joint Service Mission, and also as United Kingdom Representative on the newly formed Standing Group of the NATO Military Committee. He served there until July 1951, his status and experience enabling him to negotiate with the top Americans virtually independently, and played a major role both in planning the initial NATO command structure and representing the British view during the Korean emergency. Thereafter he divided his time between the Standard Motor Company, where he was Chairman for six years; the British Broadcasting Corporation of which he was a Governor; and the Chancellorship of Cambridge, his old University – where as CAS he had delivered his much acclaimed Lees Knowles lectures on "Air Power in Modern

War". He retained also his interest in aviation matters: in 1954, for example, he urged the formation of a National Aeronautical Collection, possibly at Hendon, and until his death in 1967 he remained connected with the Malcolm Clubs which he had helped establish during the war.

Lord Tedder was held in the highest regard by most who worked closely with him. Sir Arthur Harris considered that he had one of the most brilliant minds in any of the Services, and Maurice Dean saw him as perhaps the cleverest of all the RAF's wartime leaders, possessing great professional qualifications as a politician and a commander. Yet as Dean observes, Churchill was never entirely happy with him, and relations with Montgomery were always strained. Clearly there were differences of personality and styles of leadership, with Tedder's analytical and informal approach contrasting strongly with theirs. On the other hand, as Eisenhower recognised, it was these very qualities that enabled him to achieve so much in the fields of joint-service and Allied cooperation. Let two of the Americans who knew him best, Generals Spaatz and Eaker, have the last word: "We count it a great privilege to have had the opportunity to serve alongside one so completely dedicated to right and justice, and service to his fellow countrymen."

Marshal of the Royal Air Force Sir John Slessor

Sir John Slessor is best remembered by many as the Commander in Chief of Coastal Command at the climax of the Battle of the Atlantic, and as Chief of the Air Staff during three particularly testing post-war years. Yet he also played influential roles in much of the pre-war and wartime planning and, of all the RAF's great commanders, probably none contributed more than he to the constructive thinking about air power.

Born in India in 1897 and educated at Haileybury, Jack Slessor – as most people knew him – had suffered from polio as a boy and when the consequent lameness caused him to be rejected by the Army in 1915, he talked himself into the Royal Flying Corps; having learnt to fly at Brooklands he served briefly with 23 Squadron at Suttons Farm, where he flew his first operational sortie in a vain attempt to destroy a Zeppelin. He then joined 17 Squadron, with which he flew against the Turks in Sinai and also in the Darfur operations in the Sudan, where he was awarded the MC, wounded and invalided home. His spell as a flying instructor at Northolt was followed by further active service in France with 58 and 5 Squadrons, and during the closing stages of the war he served at the Central Flying School, Upavon.

Having briefly left the RAF in 1919 he was soon back, and while at 1 Flying Training School, Netheravon, in 1920 he took part in the first Hendon Air Display. The following year saw him join 20 Squadron at Ambala on the North West Frontier, where he was far from impressed by the Army's administrative support for the RAF's operations; in 1923 he had his first taste of the Air Ministry in the Staff Duties Branch; in 1924 he attended the RAF Staff College; and in 1925 he took command of 4 (Army Co-operation) Squadron at Farnborough. Two of the main threads in his career were thus already apparent: land/air warfare, where he was increasingly concerned at the lack of forward thinking, and high-level staff work, of which he was to have further experience from 1928-30, this time working directly under CAS in the Directorate of Operations and Intelligence. Thus began a lasting association with Trenchard, who had high regard for him and used him as ghost writer for many of his speeches, articles and letters to the press until well into the wartime years.

His Air Ministry tour cut short in 1930 by illness, Slessor's career now switched back towards the Army, with whom he spent the next four years at the Camberley Staff College, as RAF member of the Directing Staff. Although he viewed this period as a somewhat unreal existence, it provided many friendships which would later be invaluable and enabled him to develop a reputation in Service circles for clear thinking and writing, exemplified in his influential book "Air Power and Armies" published in 1936. The natural sequel to this period was a posting back to India so that he could put into practice his ideas on land/air warfare, and he commanded No 3 (Indian) Wing during the Kaisora operations in Waziristan during 1936/7. Meanwhile in 1935, soon after his arrival, he had been fortunate to survive the Quetta earthquake, having had to be rescued from the ruins of his residence.

There now began, on his return to England in 1937, a 16-year period during which he was never to be far from the centre of events. For the last years of peace, he worked first as Deputy and then Director of Plans, and he remained there – working both for CAS on the development of RAF policy and for the Chiefs of Staff as Air Member of the Joint Planning Committee – until late 1940. These were years when, as he put it, "the sense of urgency was crowding in" and, to echo John Terraine, the forthright language he used on many occasions cannot fail to impress. His anxieties about the rate of production of new aircraft and the many weaknesses of the RAF, especially in its striking power relative to the Luftwaffe, were repeatedly stated, and he could not conceive going to war at the time of Munich; Slessor was ever the realist, and he and his fellow planners worked under intense pressure to try to remedy the shortcomings, and to cope with the new problems that arose with every turn of events. Among other matters he was closely involved in the Anglo-French staff conversations of early 1939 and the many discussions between the two allies during the twilight war about how their air forces should be employed, and after a quick visit to France just before the Dunkirk evacuation he and the other British planners began at Churchill's behest to consider the strategy should France collapse. From this work stemmed their future strategy appreciation of July 1940, realistically setting forth the way in which the war should be prosecuted now that Britain and the Commonwealth stood alone*.

Since it was now clear that much American aid would be forthcoming Slessor, who had already met General Spaatz and other influential Americans in London, was sent to Washington in late 1940 to explain the RAF's plans and needs, and to negotiate for the supply of aircraft. He remained for the first full Anglo-American staff conversations about the strategy should the USA enter the conflict and as Portal's representative helped ensure a wide measure of agreement. By the time he returned home in April 1941 he was known to and respected by many of the American leaders, political as well as military.

It was time now for an operational post, and as a convinced 'bomber man' Slessor was appointed AOC 5 Group, equipped with the Hampden but soon to receive the Manchester and then the Lancaster. He stayed there only until March 1942, over a period when Bomber Command was still learning lessons the hard way and having limited material impact on the enemy, but its later achievements owed much to the patient work of its early leaders, and 5 Group would eventually play a key role in the Bomber Offensive. Slessor, however, was now needed back in the Air Ministry in the new post of Assistant Chief of Air Staff (Policy); the extension of the war to involve Russia, Japan and the USA was posing far greater planning problems than before, and his wide experience, coupled with his knowledge of the Americans, made him the ideal choice. Among the host of issues confronting him were disputes with the other Services over their air support, the allocation of American aircraft between British needs and theirs, the bombing policy to be followed by the USAAF, and

* See also page 47

the overall Anglo-American strategy; when this was considered at the Casablanca Conference in January 1943, it was Slessor's drafting for Portal that did much to reconcile the differing views.

He was now to have the chance to help implement that strategy. Crucial to the 1943 campaign in the Mediterranean and to Operation Overlord in 1944 was the defeat of the U-boat in the North Atlantic and when Slessor became CinC Coastal Command in 1943 that battle was far from won. He was, however, fortunate in that many of the techniques of naval/air warfare had at last been learnt and the long-range aircraft needed to cover the mid-ocean gap would soon be available, and his own experience both with the Royal Navy and the Americans did much to improve the co-operation between the sea and air forces on each side of the Atlantic. The great turning point in the Battle came in May, when shipping losses fell dramatically, and from then on – though Coastal Command could never relax – the U-boats were held on the defensive. Other aspects of the Command's work – photographic reconnaissance, meteorology, air sea rescue, and of increasing importance anti-shipping operations – also took Slessor's attention, and although he remained at Northwood less than a year he is widely considered the best of Coastal Command's wartime Commanders-in-Chief.

His last operational command was to be in the Mediterranean and Middle East, where in January 1944 he relieved Tedder as the RAF CinC and became deputy to his friend General Eaker as Allied Air CinC. While his purely RAF responsibilities extended right across the Middle East, much of his attention was devoted to the Italian campaign, where the maintenance of virtual air supremacy enabled the air forces to concentrate largely on the various forms of army support. Other major preoccupations were the Balkan Air Force which Slessor set up to co-ordinate air operations in support of Tito's partisan army in Yugoslavia, and the campaign to prevent a communist take-over in Greece after the German withdrawal. But it was the Warsaw Rising in the Summer of 1944 which left the deepest impression: "The worst six weeks in my experience" was how he described the supply-dropping missions from Italy which, against all his military judgement, he was for political reasons compelled to order. The cold treachery of the Russians in Poland would condition Slessor's thinking for the rest of his days.

He returned home in March 1945 to a different challenge; he was now to join the Air Council as Air Member for Personnel with the tasks of reducing the strength of the RAF from its wartime level and of rebuilding the personnel structure to fit the needs of the peacetime air force. He held the post until late in 1947, working first for Portal and then Tedder, and had to cope with all the problems connected with releasing some 700,000 airmen and airwomen to civilian life. At the same time he faced what in July 1946 he described as a well-nigh desperate recruiting situation, and the Manpower Economy Committee which he set up led eventually to a series of far-reaching measures related not just to recruiting but also to training and the overall manpower and trade structure. As might be expected, however, his interests ranged more widely: as Sir James Barnes, the Permanent Under Secretary, said in October 1947, "Slessor has made his mark on every aspect of the Council's work. His wide knowledge of the Air Force and the other Services, and his outstanding energy have not only been addressed to the work of his own Department but freely and unselfishly placed at the disposal of his colleagues in dealing with difficulties that were not strictly his own".

This enthusiasm for involving himself in all the issues of the day continued during the next two years when, as Commandant of the Imperial Defence College, he was frequently consulted by Tedder and by others in high places. The freedom from day-to-day, routine responsibilities which he saw as one of the IDC's greatest benefits, and which he was so keen to preserve, gave him personally the opportunity to think deeply about the strategic problems of the post-war world and the roles of air power in the nuclear age - a good preparation for his final RAF posting.

Sir John Slessor became CAS on 1 January 1950, having just completed a world tour to bring himself up to date, and his three years in post were dominated by the Korean War and its repercussions. In the situation which ensued from the invasion of South Korea on 25 June 1950, he himself was reminded of the Munich crisis of 1938, when Britain's defences had seemed just as inadequate, and he immediately asked his staff to consider how the RAF's capacity could be improved should the financial constraints be lifted. At the same time he gave his Chiefs of Staff colleagues a strong lead in insisting that the Soviet threat in the west remained paramount; with every effort now being made to establish the NATO military structure and build up its forces (a process in which he was closely concerned), Korea must not be allowed to weaken that position. The RAF in particular, with key roles in Western Europe and already deeply committed in the Malayan Emergency, could not possibly play a significant part in Korea, though Slessor did provide some Sunderland squadrons and a number of the RAF's best pilots to fly with the Americans and the Australians. He himself, however, played an important role, particularly when the Chinese Air Force joined in the war from Manchuria and General MacArthur demanded permission to attack their bases. In the view of the British Government and the Chiefs of Staff this would cause a dangerous escalation of the war, and in January 1951 he was chosen by the Cabinet to go to Washington to explain to the American leaders Britain's anxieties about the military situation and the dangers to Anglo-American solidarity. In the event the war was contained and if the United Kingdom exercised a restraining influence as it almost certainly did, then Slessor deserves his share of the credit.

Nevertheless, as he himself said, the possibility of war with the Soviet Union in the next few years still loomed large, and much of his time as CAS was devoted to strengthening the RAF under the major re-armament programme instituted by the Attlee Government. While the development of the new advanced aircraft such as the V-bombers was pressed forward, the urgent need was for many more aircraft in the short term; the Washington and Sabre supplied by the USA filled the immediate gap, and an order was placed for a force of over 600 Canberras, which started to enter service in 1951. A host of other issues also engaged his attention, such as the expansion of flying training, flying accident rates, the restoration of the UK control and reporting system, the deployment of the USAF on British bases, the LAA defence of overseas airfields, air support for the Army, the re-equipment of the transport force, the introduction of the first helicopters, and not least the first British atomic tests.

34 *The Allied air commanders in the Mediterranean theatre, April 1943. Left to right: Air Vice Marshal 'Mary' Coningham, General Spaatz, USAAF, Air Marshal Tedder, General Kuter, USAAF.*

35 *Sir Arthur Tedder greets Sir John Slessor on his arrival in North Africa, January 1944.*

36 *The Allied commanders at a pre-invasion meeting, February 1944. Left to right: General Bradley, Admiral Ramsay, Air Chief Marshal Tedder, General Eisenhower, General Montgomery, Air Chief Marshal Leigh-Mallory, General Bedell Smith.*

37 *The Air Council in 1949. Left to right: Air Marshal Sir Alec Coryton (Controller of Supplies (Air)), Air Marshal Sir Arthur Sanders (VCAS), Air Marshal Sir Hugh Saunders (AMP), MRAF The Lord Tedder (CAS), The Rt Hon Arthur Henderson (Secretary of State for Air), Mr Geoffrey de Freitas (US of S for Air), Sir James Barnes (PUS), Air Chief Marshal Sir George Pirie (AMSO), Mr H T Smith (Clerk to the Air Council), Mr A L H Cary (Private Secretary to S of S).*

38 Sir John Slessor, as AMP, is welcomed by Air Chief Marshal Sir Keith Park in Singapore, April 1946.

39 Sir John Slessor uses one of the RAF's earliest helicopters, a Sycamore, to visit Rugby School, July 1952.

40 Sir John Slessor welcomes General Ridgway, Supreme Allied Commander Europe, a few days later.

41 Sir William Dickson and his fellow Chiefs of Staff, Admiral of the Fleet Sir Roderick McGrigor and General Sir John Harding, ready to ride in the Queen's Coronation Procession, 1953.

42 Sir William Dickson accompanies Marshal Tito at the Duxford Air Display, March 1953.

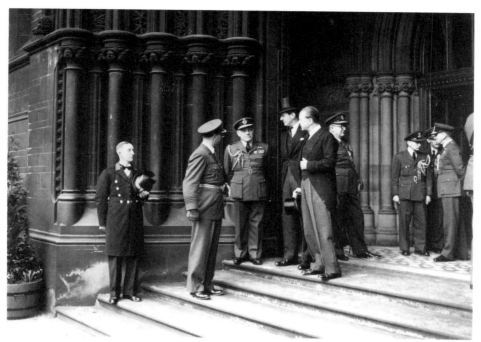

43 *Sir William Dickson in Manchester, after the Queen's Colour for the RAF had been presented for the first time with full ceremonial in any provincial city, April 1953.*

44 *Air Vice-Marshal Boyle, as AOC 1 Group, meets Air Commodore Bufton, Squadron Leader Mountford and Group Captain Hyde after a Canberra exercise.*

45 *Sir Dermot Boyle welcomes the Queen and the Duke of Edinburgh to RAF Marham, July 1956. On Sir Dermot's left are Air Marshal Sir Harry Broadhurst (CinC Bomber Command), Air Vice Marshal Sir John Whitley (AOC 1 Group), Air Vice-Marshal Cross (AOC 3 Group) and Group Captain Hodges (OC Marham).*

46 *Distinguished company at a Guest Night at Headquarters Strike Command, August 1973. Left to right: Sir George Edwards (Chairman of the British Aircraft Corporation), Sir Denis Spotswood (CAS), Mr Anthony Kershaw (US of S (Air)), Sir Andrew Humphrey (AOCinC Strike Command), Sir Dermot Boyle.*

*47 Sir Thomas Pike, AOCinC
Fighter Command, greets the
Luftwaffe's General
Kammhuber, October 1956 –
an interesting meeting between
a distinguished RAF night
fighter pilot and the man who
had organised the German
night fighter defences in World
War II.*

*48 Sir Thomas Pike, with Mr Julian Amery (Secretary of State for Air), greets Major Gagarin, the
Soviet astronaut, July 1961.*

49 *Sir Thomas Pike represents the Royal Air Force at the unveiling of the statue of Lord Trenchard in Whitehall Gardens, July 1961. The Archbishop of Canterbury, the Most Reverend The Lord Ramsay, leads the group, followed by the Prime Minister, Mr Harold Macmillan, and Mr Julian Amery. On CAS's right is the Second Lord Trenchard, who up to his recent death gave much support to this book.*

50 *Lord Dowding and Sir Thomas Pike visit the restored Operations Room of Headquarters 11 Group at RAF Uxbridge, April 1958.*

Slessor handed over the reins at the end of 1952 and thereafter devoted much of his time until his death in 1979 to writing and the defence debate. "The Central Blue", which appeared in 1956, still stands as the best book written by a former CAS, and by speaking at conferences, being interviewed on the radio, and writing a multitude of papers, articles and letters for the Press, he constantly sought to influence opinion at home and abroad on air power and wider defence issues. In so doing he kept in close touch with his successors, frequently offering advice and sometimes acting as their unofficial spokesman. Certainly Slessor deserves recognition as one of the great thinkers about air strategy, and he also proved himself to be one of the RAF's most able operational commanders. Above all, however, he had the staff skills and the ability to get on with leaders at the highest level which proved their worth both in wartime and in dealing with the special challenges that faced him as Chief of the Air Staff.

Marshal of the Royal Air Force
Sir William Dickson

Unlike his predecessors as CAS, all of whom had begun their flying careers in the Royal Flying Corps, Sir William Dickson started out as a Naval airman, hardly surprising for a great-great grandson of Lord Nelson. He also finished his service career in unique fashion, as the first and only full-time Chairman of the Chiefs of Staff and then for a brief spell as the first Chief of the Defence Staff. Thus, having flown on operations before the third Service was formed, he was closely concerned in the first major moves, over 40 years later, to bring the three Services under strong central direction.

William Dickson was born in 1898. When the war started in 1914 he was at Haileybury and his inclinations towards the Navy, combined with a fascination in flying engendered by a visit to Hendon, led him to join the Royal Naval Air Service in October 1916. His training to fly seaplanes, first at Lake Windermere and then at Calshot, took five months, whereupon he went to the Isle of Grain to fly anti-submarine patrols and make some unsuccessful attempts to intercept German Gothas. Then in June 1917 he was chosen for the complement of the new aircraft carrier HMS Furious, which joined the Grand Fleet in order to provide fighter protection against the Zeppelins; soon realising the disadvantages of having to touch down in the sea he was one of the early pioneers of deck landings, and later took part in the first carrier-based bombing raid, against a Zeppelin base at Tondern.

The end of the war found him serving aboard HMS Revenge, and in August 1919, while Fleet Aviation Officer on HMS Queen Elizabeth, he was awarded his permanent commission in the RAF. Now somewhat disenchanted with the attitude of the Navy's senior officers towards aircraft, he was quickly persuaded of the need for the independent air force and over the next few years, having completed a flying instructor course at Gosport with Smith-Barry, he did some experimental deck flying and served a spell as a test pilot at Farnborough. Then in 1923, his flying tour cut short by a motor-cycle accident, he was posted to the Air Ministry as the sole Flight Lieutenant in Trenchard's small team, where he doubled as PA to Sir John Steele, DCAS, and as the expert on naval/air operations. This was no easy task at a time when Trenchard, who himself knew little about fleet aviation, was having to fight to prevent its return to the Navy, and Dickson not only learnt much but established his reputation as a clever staff officer.

In 1926, he joined 56 Squadron at Biggin Hill, where his return to flying gave him great delight; 1928 he spent as a student at the Staff College; and in 1929 he went abroad to India. For a year he served on the North West Frontier, gaining his first experience of working with the Army in air control operations designed to keep the local tribes in order; thereafter he served under Sir Geoffrey Salmond at Headquarters India, which gave him the opportunity to fly over much of South East Asia as far as Singapore. He returned home in 1934, spent 1935 commanding a Fury squadron, No 25, at Hawkinge, and then joined the directing staff at the RAF Staff College, before attending the Imperial Defence College in 1939. Thus by the outbreak of war he had not only wide flying experience and considerable knowledge of the other Services but also well developed staff skills; he was thus an obvious choice for appointment to the Directorate of Plans, where he would work under Slessor on the Joint Planning Staff*.

The immediate task for him and his colleagues in September 1939 was to set up a new strategic planning section, which included establishing the map room and recruiting retired officers to assist. They then devoted their attention essentially to forward planning, and among their main concerns in the early months was the long series of staff conversations with the French, whose confidence in their ability to defend themselves was not entirely shared by Dickson and his colleagues. Much time was spent too on planning the Narvik operation in Northern Norway. Then in May 1940, as Dickson recalled, the direction and pace of the whole machine changed with the Battle of France and the arrival of Churchill. Policy and plans were now formulated right at the top and the planners found themselves working directly for the Chiefs of Staff and so under intense pressure. Their biggest task was to compile the comprehensive future strategy paper, and Dickson had no doubt that its central feature must be the strategic air offensive; for him this offered the only means of reducing Germany's overwhelming land power and thus making possible the eventual return to Europe.

Such was his success in this appointment that in March 1941 he was chosen to take over from Slessor as Director of Plans, and after Hitler attacked Russia in June – an act of suicide, Dickson called it – he took part in meetings with the Soviet Ambassador to explain the military aid that could be offered, which was of course far less than was being requested. He was still there when the USA entered the war in December, and he and his Navy and Army colleagues accompanied the Prime Minister to the Arcadia Conference at which the joint strategy was discussed. Dickson, who attended the Combined Chiefs of Staff meetings, remembered in particular the furious arguments about policy, the way the US Army Air Corps was so completely subordinated to the Army, and the poor quality of the American committee work, but he also noticed one remarkably able planner in the person of Brigadier Eisenhower.

It was now time for a change and in April 1942 Dickson went to Fighter Command, first as SASO and then AOC 9 Group at Preston, where he could pick up the techniques of fighter defence. Six months later he moved to Rudloe Manor to become AOC 10 Group, which covered much of Southern England and had not only to meet a continuing, though limited, Luftwaffe threat, but also to escort the increasing daylight offensive against Northern France, and in March 1943 General Eaker singled out Dickson for his co-operation in the development of Anglo-American operations. By this time much of the preparation for Overlord was being set in train and since many of Fighter Command's squadrons would be needed for offensive operations Dickson was switched to the newly formed 83 Group which would form part of the Second Tactical Air

* See page 42

Force for the invasion. He spent the next year organising the Group and making it ready, only to be told in early 1944 that he was to hand it over to Harry Broadhurst and take over the Desert Air Force in Italy instead; as Portal explained to Dickson, Montgomery had insisted on bringing with him from Italy the air commanders whom he knew.

So from April until December 1944 Dickson served again under Slessor, leading an Air Force which was at this stage of the war highly experienced and efficient; co-operation with the 12th USAAF was excellent, and since the Luftwaffe was now relatively ineffective, the two air forces could concentrate largely on interdiction and close support for the land forces fighting their way North. The intensity and variety of the air operations, together with the complex inter-Service and inter-Allied relationships, made this a challenging front-line appointment, but Dickson had held it for a mere nine months when to his great disappointment Portal recalled him to the Air Ministry. Here, as Assistant Chief of Air Staff (Policy), he became involved in a host of matters as the European war drew to its close, with the preparations to send an RAF bomber force to the Far East to join in the assault on Japan among the most important. He was thus well aware of the awful cost likely to be entailed in overthrowing her, and when he heard the news that Japan had surrendered he could only applaud the decision to use the atomic bomb.

Dickson remained ACAS (Pol) until June 1946, when Tedder chose him to join the Air Council as Vice Chief of Air Staff. While the continuing tensions in many parts of the world engaged some of his attention, there was much to do in preparing the RAF's re-equipment programme – the Operational Requirements for the V-bombers were, for example, issued at this time – and renewed pressure by the Navy to take over Coastal Command had to be resisted. Working with Tedder, who was always accessible and a great decentraliser, was easy and it was with mixed feelings that Dickson left the Air Ministry in March 1948 for Ismailia to become Commander-in-Chief RAF Middle East. His responsibilities here covered a vast area extending as far as the Gulf, Aden, Kenya and the Sudan, and while his eight AOCs handled the operational problems in their respective areas Dickson's Headquarters had to provide all the administrative and technical support and run the Command's extensive air transport service. He himself remained largely behind the scenes, exercising general supervision, liaising closely with the other Commanders-in-Chief and spending much time visiting his many bases and staging posts, but in January 1949, after the British withdrawal from Palestine, he assumed personal control when the Government called for aerial photographs in order to convince the Americans that Israeli forces had crossed the frontier into Sinai. Unfortunately four RAF Spitfires were shot down during the consequent reconnaissance missions but when Dickson came under fire in Parliament he was firmly defended by the Prime Minister, Clement Attlee, over what had been essentially a political air operation.

He returned home in early 1950 to work again under Slessor, this time as AMSO, and a year later the post of Air Member for Technical Services was abolished and its functions combined with his. With responsibilities now ranging from organisation, works and supply to repair and maintenance, he was thus deeply involved in the expansion programme ordered by the Government at the time of the Korean War. The biggest problem as he recollected was the supply of aircraft, caused by the limited capacity of the aviation industry, and while every effort was made to raise the production of current types it was also decided to buy the Sabre from the USA. At the same time planning for the deployment of a large USAF contingent in the United Kingdom entailed the selection of many new bases, and the terms on which these were provided were embodied in a formal agreement between Dickson and his American opposite number, General Johnson. Other matters engaging his concern included a massive building programme extending from airfields to domestic accommodation, readjustment of the RAF's command structure, restoration of the control and reporting system, re-equipment of the transport force, and the problems of replacing the Sunderland; as a former Naval airman, Dickson was all for retaining the flying boat.

So it was as a seasoned and up-to-date Whitehall warrior that Dickson undertook his world tour before taking over from Slessor as Chief of the Air Staff in January 1953. Churchill, who was again Prime Minister and liked to retain close ties with his Chiefs of Staff, remembered him as one of his wartime planners and Dickson was well supported in all the planning and preparation for the RAF's nuclear deterrent force, which was seen as the future cornerstone of the nation's defences. It was this task, the establishment of the V-force and the weapons, airfields and trained personnel that went with it, that was his main preoccupation, and although a reduction in the size of the force from 240 to 144 had to be accepted, by the time he left office the Medium Bomber Force was firmly on the stocks. Moreover, thanks in part to Dickson's strong encouragement, the USAF presence was soundly re-established in the United Kingdom.

At the same time, however, the Government was re-appraising the likely Soviet strategy in the aftermath of Korea, and with defence expenditure – fuelled by the current expansion programme – climbing rapidly, a major defence review was in prospect. Since in Dickson's view much emphasis must in future be placed on cold war operations, the Air Staff gave much thought to the role of Transport Command and the aircraft it would need; the Vickers 1000, for example, was considered and rejected, and the Britannia ordered. At the same time the introduction of the first helicopters caused the opening of the long-running debate with the Army about their control. Other problems engaging Dickson's attention included the cancellation of the Swift, aircraft accident rates, the future of the Royal Auxiliary Air Force flying squadrons, and an expected shortage of pilots and navigators, and in 1955 the Hollinghurst Committee's proposals to reduce substantially the Group Headquarters staffs were implemented*.

Dickson could normally have expected to depart in December 1955, but Eden – now Prime Minister – had decided to strengthen the Ministry of Defence in relation to the Service Ministries by appointing a separate Chairman of the Chiefs of Staff to act as the Defence Minister's Military Adviser. Recognising the increasingly important role of the RAF and encouraged by Mountbatten, who was keen on the new arrangement, Eden offered Dickson the new post, which he held throughout the Suez crisis and the Sandys Defence Review. Despite being ill at times during Suez he played his part in

See also page 58

ensuring the success of the military operations, even though he doubted their wisdom, but during the bitter Chiefs of Staffs debates over Sandys' proposals he was unable to exercise much influence; consequently, as a great believer in the need for a stronger 'centre', he supported Macmillan's proposal in 1958 to convert his post to Chief of the Defence Staff, and once the decision had been made in face of strong opposition, he took on the new job, handing over to Mountbatten in early 1959.

In retirement his interests included the Royal Central Asian Society, the Ex-Services Mental Welfare Society, and the Forces Help Society and Lord Roberts Workshops, and he was always prepared to take up the cudgels on behalf of his old Service through the correspondence columns of the press. The last of the RAF's Chiefs to have served in the First World War, he died in 1987. Never afraid to speak his mind and a firm advocate of air power, Sir William Dickson was also a great believer in joint-Service co-operation; there could have been no better choice for the first Chief of the Defence Staff.

Marshal of the Royal Air Force Sir Dermot Boyle

When Sir Dermot Boyle was appointed Chief of the Air Staff on 1 January 1956 nobody was more delighted than Lord Trenchard, who had always looked forward to the day when the first officer to have received his training at the RAF College which he had founded would reach the highest position the Service had to offer. Trenchard died soon afterwards – indeed the new CAS's first public engagement was to attend his funeral – but had he lived long enough to see the way in which the raison d'être of the RAF was now to be challenged he would have been proud of the man whose leadership was about to be put to the test.

Dermot Boyle was born and bred in Ireland, where he attended school in Dublin. In 1922, at the age of 18, he decided that instead of remaining at home to help run the family estate he wanted to learn to fly, and that a cadetship at the recently established RAF College at Cranwell offered a very good way of doing so. During his time there, as he recalls, he was greatly impressed with his instructors and the way the training was organised, and he became totally dedicated to the RAF; indeed these two formative years were to condition all his thinking and ever since he has been one of the strongest advocates of the traditional Cranwell system.

Having graduated in July 1924 he was posted to 17 Squadron at Hawkinge, where he flew the Snipe, and then at the end of 1925 he went to Iraq, where he spent a year at Hinaidi with 1 Squadron on air policing duties, and then a few months at Mosul with 6 Squadron, thus gaining invaluable experience of operational flying and seeing how a front-line squadron should be run. He returned home in early 1927, qualified as a flying instructor, and next served at the Central Flying School until the end of 1929; this gave him the opportunity to carry out some display flying and he and Dick (Batchy) Atcherley made names for themselves with their aerobatics. 1930 saw a welcome return to Cranwell, again as a flying instructor, after which he went to Hendon as Adjutant of 601 Squadron. In this appointment he was not only CO in all but name but also became convinced of the value of the Auxiliary Air Force, not least because it gave civilians – often influential – intimate knowledge of the RAF and thus won their support. George Ward, who later became his Secretary of State for Air, was one such whom he always quotes.

In 1933 he went abroad again, this time to HQ India, where for almost three years he became immersed in the administration of airmen's personal affairs – for a pilot an initially unattractive task that he later realised had given him a superb insight into a mundane but fundamental aspect of Service life. There followed a year at the Staff College in 1936, again entered on with some reluctance but yielding skills, contacts and experience that he subsequently recognised as invaluable. Immediately afterwards he took command of the recently re-formed 83 Squadron, based at Turnhouse and equipped with the Hawker Hind light bomber, but a mere seven months later his instructional experience was again in demand and he returned to Cranwell, this time as Chief Flying Instructor. He thus had a key role as the intensity of the flying training programme built up and the College re-organised on the approach of war, and of the cadets taught to fly during his time many were to distinguish themselves and many to lose their lives.

It was in November 1939 that he left Cranwell to join the Headquarters of the Advanced Air Striking Force in Rheims as Wing Commander Administrative Plans, and when the German Army broke through in May 1940 it was he who had to arrange the evacuation of the force via Brest; surprisingly in retrospect the biggest problem to be overcome was not the Luftwaffe but the flood of refugees that clogged the roads. On returning home he was sent to the Operations Staff at Headquarters Bomber Command, where he worked first for Portal and then Peirse during the earliest days of the strategic bomber offensive, and in November 1940 he was reappointed to command 83 Squadron, now based at Scampton and equipped with the Hampden. Delighted to have the opportunity to command a squadron in war, he flew his first operational sortie on 3 January 1941, against Bremen, following up in February with two more against Dusseldorf and Wilhelmshaven; then to his total surprise he was summoned by Portal to join the select team of senior officers that worked in the Cabinet Office Secretariat. So for the next year, far from being in the thick of the battle where he would have wished to be, he was caught up in the higher realms of policy-making as Secretary to a number of committees, one of them chaired by the Minister of Aircraft Production, Moore-Brabazon, and concerned with the early stages of the development of the atomic bomb.

In January 1942, however, he returned to the front line taking command of RAF Stradishall, one of Bomber Command's main airfields, and over the following months his squadrons, notably 214 equipped first with the Wellington and then the Stirling, played their full part in the mounting strategic air offensive against Germany. On occasion he himself flew with them and on 2 June 1942, after the first thousand bomber raids, he issued a much appreciated Special Order of the Day thanking all the men and women on his station for their contributions to these highly successful attacks. Among other units at Stradishall during his time were 109 Squadron, whose Wellingtons were flying special radio reconnaissance missions and participating in the 'Window' trials, and 138 Squadron which carried out special duties operations with its Whitleys. Late in 1942 Stradishall changed roles, becoming the home of 1657 Heavy Conversion Unit, and early the next year Boyle was on his way again, this time to 83 Group as Senior Air Staff Officer. 83 Group had been newly created, initially in Fighter Comand, and the 29 Spitfire, Typhoon and Mustang squadrons it would soon acquire were to form part of the 2nd Tactical Air Force for the invasion of North West Europe. Boyle, who had had first-hand experience of the German use of tactical air power in the Battle of France, was an ideal choice to serve under William Dickson in the all-important planning phase, and when Dickson was replaced by Harry Broadhurst in early 1944 Boyle stayed on. He thus became involved in directing the increasingly intensive air operations against targets in Northern France in the months before D-Day and subsequently during the invasion campaign itself and the advance into Germany. Reflecting later, he particularly recalls the almost complete air superiority possessed by the RAF and USAAF, together with the total surprise achieved by the Luftwaffe in Operation Bodenplatte, its mass attack on the Allied airfields on 1 January 1945. Altogether he spent almost two years in this key operational post, and in April 1945 he became for a few months AOC 85 Group, responsible for the multiplicity of support units within the 2nd Tactical Air Force, which was now taking over the British Occupation Zone of Germany.

There followed a short tour as AOC 11 Group, cut short by his selection to attend the Imperial Defence College in 1946, after which he was appointed Assistant Commandant at the RAF Staff College. The opportunities thus provided to reflect on wartime experiences, to think about the future, and to meet and get to know people of widely differing backgrounds proved invaluable, and in 1948 he returned to the Air Ministry to work first as Director General of Personnel and then Director General of Manning. His earlier experience of looking after airmen's affairs in India now stood him in particularly good stead and for nearly three years he was involved in the difficult personnel problems that stemmed from the post-war contraction of the RAF and the need for renewed expansion as the Soviet threat became increasingly apparent. Not least of his many concerns was the policy for the new National Service scheme.

By 1951 he was ready for a return to operational command and in April, after a short flying refresher course, he took over as AOC 1 Group in Bomber Command, where an exciting challenge awaited him, that of seeing the RAF's first jet bomber into service. During his two years at Bawtry his initial force of eight Lincoln and two Mosquito squadrons would change shape radically as the new Canberra force was built up; the first aircraft to reach Bomber Command arrived at Binbrook in May and by 1953 eight squadrons of the new light bomber were operational in 1 Group. Boyle himself often flew this wonderful aircraft, as he called it, most notably in late 1952 when he led a flight of four Canberras on a 24,000 mile trip round most of the countries of South America.

His penultimate appointment came in April 1953 when he became AOC-in-C Fighter Command, just in time to take charge of the Queen's Coronation Review at Odiham on 15 July, when over 600 aircraft took part in what he proudly described as "a model flypast". At this time Fighter Command was largely equipped with the Meteor and the Vampire, but during the next couple of years he was to preside over the introduction of the first 12 squadrons of the next generation of the jet fighter, the Hunter. At the same time he realised that reductions in the strength of the Command were inevitable before much longer, though there was little sign of the fearsome cutbacks that would be inflicted on the United Kingdom's air defences while he was Chief of the Air Staff.

Sir Dermot Boyle took over from Sir William Dickson on 1 January 1956; unusually for a CAS he had never served on the Air Council but in this he saw no disadvantage, nor was he embarrassed about his predecessor remaining as Chairman of the Chiefs of Staff – though he was apprehensive about the longer term implications of this move towards greater centralisation and suspicious of the motives of Lord Mountbatten, his Naval opposite number. He held the post for four years, a period remembered on two special counts: the Suez Crisis and the Sandys Defence Review.

Suez dominated the second half of 1956, with the various stages of military planning and preparations, compounded by the political uncertainties, occupying much of the attention of the Chiefs of Staff. Boyle himself refused to become involved in the political aspects and knew nothing of the Israel connections, though he certainly shared his colleagues' misgivings about a situation in which Eden was being steadily overwhelmed. His task was simply to ensure that the RAF could do what was required of it, and he shares the credit for his Service's success in Operation Musketeer, in cooperation with the Fleet Air Arm and the French Air Force.

The Sandys Review presented problems of a different order. The major re-assessment of British defence policy started in fact in early 1956, its cause the Government's conviction that Britain's economic performance had to be improved and that major savings in expenditure on conventional forces were essential to that end. After Suez the painful process was resumed, this time under a new Minister of Defence, Duncan Sandys, and the Defence White Paper of April 1957 caused consternation around the RAF. Admittedly Boyle applauded one key aspect, the confirmation of the role of the V-bomber force in providing the United Kingdom's nuclear deterrent, in which he was a passionate believer. But in predicting that the advent of the missile would mean the end of the manned fighter aircraft – an idea which, as Boyle said, came out of Sandys' head – the Minister was presenting the RAF with a challenge to its very existence. Quickly realising that resignation on this issue would serve no purpose, Boyle decided to fight; while heavy cuts had to be accepted, especially in Fighter Command and Germany, he found many influential friends, notably in the Army and also in politics, willing to support him and, as he put it, the fabric of the RAF as a whole was preserved; moreover – a major achievement – he persuaded Sandys to agree to the development of the TSR2. At the same time he realised the importance of countering the effects of the adverse publicity both within and outside the RAF, and by repeatedly proclaiming his own belief in the future of the manned aircraft he made a major personal contribution to the national debate; for those in the RAF, increasingly wondering about their prospects, his was a timely demonstration of inspired leadership.

Many other matters, too, engaged his attention, including an attempt by the Navy, strongly encouraged by Mountbatten when he became Chief of the Defence Staff, to take over the aircraft of Coastal Command, and a full-scale study of the future roles of air transport. In the nuclear field there were the successful tests of the British hydrogen bomb at Christmas Island; the agreement to the deployment of the Thor missile in the United Kingdom – a decision which Boyle supported since it brought the RAF into a new field of technology and would help prepare for the advent of Britain's intercontinental ballistic missile, Blue Streak; and the growing question mark about Blue Streak itself, coupled with the possible acquisition of the air-launched Skybolt instead. When he handed over at the end of 1959 there remained many unsolved questions but the RAF was in much better heart than at one stage had seemed possible.

He was now aged 55 and new challenges lay ahead, both in industry and in continuing connections with the Royal Air Force. As Vice-Chairman of the British Aircraft Corporation from 1962-1971 his Service experience was invaluable for many of the new aircraft projects; the cancellations, especially that of the TSR2, horrified him, but other projects such as the MRCA held great hopes for the future. Alongside this work he found time for a new scheme very close to his own heart, namely the establishment of the Royal Air Force's own Museum at Hendon; as the first Chairman of its Board of Trustees from 1965-1974 he provided much of the guidance and inspiration for this widely admired RAF institution. The RAF Benevolent Fund of which he was Vice-Chairman for most of the 1970s, and the RAF Club of which he was President for many years, also owe him much, and he has continued to show an active interest in many aspects of modern RAF activity, still offering advice and encouragement wherever appropriate.

Of all the great RAF institutions with which he has been connected, however, Cranwell retains the strongest hold on his affections, and while he appreciates the reasons for its changed role he remains firmly convinced that the Cranwell system which moulded him should never have been abandoned.

Marshal of the Royal Air Force
Sir Thomas Pike

Sir Thomas Pike had what some might have thought a narrow range of experience for a Chief of the Air Staff, his career having been largely concentrated in the fighter world, flying instruction, and operational requirements. Yet in his 3½ years in office he led the RAF safely through a period when there were many question marks about its future, and afterwards – uniquely for a former CAS – went on to become Deputy Supreme Allied Commander Europe.

Tom Pike was born in Lewisham on 29 June 1906 and, after being educated at Bedford School, was accepted for a cadetship at the RAF College Cranwell commencing on 1 January 1924. He enjoyed his time there, making many life-long friends, but while he thought the discipline and training were first-class he was less impressed by the standard of flying instruction in those early days. His two years at Cranwell complete, he joined 56 Fighter Squadron, well known as the squadron of Ball and McCudden, in January 1926 and for the next three years flew Grebes at Biggin Hill and later Siskins at North Weald. At the end of 1928 he was chosen to become a flying instructor, and having first been taught, as he put it, "to fly properly and to teach others", he spent 1929 and 1930 first at 5 Flying Training School Sealand, and then at the Central Flying School Wittering, where he was a member of the Aerobatic Team, flying the Gypsy Moth.

In August 1930 came a new challenge when he went to Henlow to undertake the two-year Long Engineering Course, after which he was posted to the Middle East Depot at Aboukir on engineering duties. A return to flying instruction followed, this time at 4 Flying Training School Abu Sueir, and he returned home at the end of 1936 to attend 15 Course at the RAF Staff College, Andover. He might now have expected a change of role, but with the Service expanding rapidly as the threat of war grew his experience of flying training was again required, this time as Chief Flying Instructor at 10 Flying Training School, Ternhill. A year later, however, in February 1939, he was sent to the Air Ministry in the Directorate of Organisation, where he remained until early 1941, concerned with some of the urgent problems of the RAF's wartime expansion.

The frustration felt by a man of his background at being divorced from the scene of action during 1940 can well be imagined, but his chance came early in 1941. As a Wing Commander he was now appointed to command 219 Squadron, which had just been re-equipped with the AI-fitted Beaufighter for the night fighter role and was based at Tangmere, also the home of the day fighter wing led by Douglas Bader, with whom he struck up a close friendship. The cities of the United Kingdom were still under heavy Luftwaffe attack, and – as stated in the citation for the Distinguished Flying Cross that he was soon to receive – Tom Pike showed great skill in intercepting enemy aircraft at night.

He destroyed a Heinkel on his first patrol and soon afterwards shot down at least three more, two on one night. His keenness and example had a splendid effect on the other members of the squadron, who promptly nicknamed him 'Killer', and after a mere six months he was again promoted to take over responsibility for night operations at Headquarters 11 Group.

He was still not to be left long in one place: early in 1942 he took command of the fighter station at North Weald; later that year he returned to 11 Group as Senior Officer Administration; and in mid-1943 he moved to the Mediterranean theatre to command No 1 Mobile Operations Room during the Allied landings in Italy and the early stages of the subsequent campaign. Then in February 1944 he became Senior Air Staff Officer at Headquarters Desert Air Force, working under his former flight commander, William Dickson, and he remained in Italy for the rest of the war, responsible for the RAF's activities in close support of the 8th Army during its northward advance. This gave him invaluable experience of joint operations, and the opportunity to work for the first time with the Americans was later to stand him in good stead; the award of the Legion of Merit indicated the high opinion they had of him.

The first year after the war he spent in command of No 1 Officers' Advanced Training School, briefly at Cranwell and then at Digby, after which he returned to the Air Ministry as Director of Operational Requirements. His two years there he found particularly challenging, since he was closely concerned with the development of the new generation of aircraft that would replace the wartime types, but as he later reflected nobody appreciated that British industry was no longer capable of producing two or three different aircraft to meet each specification in order that the RAF could then choose the best. Even so the foundations for several RAF success stories were well laid during his time, most notably the V-bombers and – an aircraft much after his own heart – the Hunter.

1949 saw him attending the course at the Imperial Defence College, whereupon he was posted yet again to 11 Group at Hillingdon, this time as AOC. Largely equipped with the Meteor and Vampire, plus the Mosquito in the night fighter role, this famous Group – though much reduced in strength compared with wartime days – was still responsible for the air defence of most of southern England and the threat of Soviet attack could not be taken lightly in a period marked by continued tension in Europe and the onset of the Korean War. This spell of operational command was followed in mid-1951 by his appointment as Deputy Chief of Staff (Operations) at Headquarters Allied Air Forces Central Europe, Fontainebleau, working for General Norstad; while these were the formative years of NATO and might have been considered particularly demanding, he himself found his time in Europe disappointing: always a hard worker he thought the staffs were overlarge and had too little to do. It was therefore to his relief that he returned home two years later to join the Air Council as Deputy Chief of Air Staff – a post for which Air Vice-Marshal Brook had been designated before his death in a flying accident.

Tom Pike was well fitted for his new job, not least by virtue of his time in Operational Requirements, and for the next three years working again under Sir William Dickson he was responsible, as he put it, for the RAF's hardware*.

* See page 49

Perhaps his most difficult decision was to advise the Air Council that the Swift was unacceptable for operational service and could never be made satisfactory, but the Hunter went ahead and the initial orders for the Lightning were placed. The re-equipment of the long-range transport force was another major preoccupation and although the VC1000 which he favoured had to be cancelled the Britannia was ordered instead. The modernisation of the United Kingdom GEE system, the introduction of surface-to-air missiles for air defence, the development of Blue Steel in order to extend the life of the V-bombers, and the planning for the Christmas Island atomic trials were among the many other matters that came his way, and by the middle of the 1956 he was ready to return to Fighter Command, this time as Commander-in-Chief.

Sadly, however, his three years at Bentley Priory coincided with the Sandys Defence Review, as a result of which the United Kingdom's fighter defences were sharply cut back and the Royal Auxiliary Air Force squadrons that had played such an important role in them abolished. Tom Pike himself refused to become depressed by the situation and concentrated on preserving the essentials of the Air Defence System and ensuring its public image – not least through the display activities of 92 and 111 Squadrons, widely known as the Blue Diamonds and the Black Arrows. As he later reflected, however, nothing could change the blinkered attitude of Duncan Sandys whose conviction that manned fighter aircraft had no future made it impossible for anyone to reason with him. Even when Sandys visited Fighter Command for a major exercise in which Pike's aircraft were remarkably successful he refused to accept the evidence. It was maybe just as well that Sandys had departed when Tom Pike was appointed Chief of the Air Staff on 1 January 1960.

He held the post for more than 3½ years, a period when – despite the sterling work of his predecessor – there were great doubts about the long-term future of the RAF. Undoubtedly its current roles were highly important, centring on Bomber Command which was a remarkably efficient force charged with providing the United Kingdom's nuclear deterrent. The Service also had major tasks overseas, in the Mediterranean, Middle and Far East, and in Tom Pike's time it played important roles in the operations in support of Kuwait in 1961*, the Brunei emergency of 1962 and the early months of Confrontation with Indonesia. Yet there were increasing signs that Britain's world-wide commitments were more than she could sustain and Pike – always a believer in the need to retain fixed bases overseas – argued firmly against those who urged withdrawal and if necessary forcing one's way back in. Elsewhere too the pressures were strong: the Blue Streak strategic missile system on which so many hopes had been based as the successor to the V-bombers had to be cancelled when the accuracy of the new Soviet missiles was appreciated; then the Americans cancelled the Skybolt project and Britain decided instead to turn to the Polaris system. This was a body blow to Tom Pike and the RAF, and growing doubts about the viability of the TSR 2 on cost grounds only made things worse; as he himself said: "It was a splendid aircraft but the RAF was asking too much".

There were other anxieties too. The ending of National Service was causing major recruiting problems and while he saw that the RAF would be

* See page 62

more efficient as a volunteer force – provided the pay was right – he thought it should have been retained for the sake of the nation as a whole. Then there were the growing pressures for a stronger central defence structure which culminated in the decision announced in March 1963 to establish a unified Ministry of Defence; Tom Pike – a firm believer in the merits of the traditional Chiefs of Staff system – disliked this, fought against it, and remained convinced that it was inefficient.

But if his years as CAS were particularly difficult, that was no fault of his. The political and economic pressures, not to mention those from Mountbatten, Chief of the Defence Staff, and the other Services, were such as to require a strong hand if the RAF was to be protected, and once he had taken time to consider his views he always presented them firmly and clearly. Not for him the machinations and deviousness that seemed to him to characterise the politicians and some of his military colleagues; he was essentially a straightforward, honest man who in his quiet way inspired the confidence of the men and women he led. "RAF News", which he instituted as a newspaper for the RAF about the RAF, may perhaps stand as one tribute to a CAS who believed deeply in the Service to which he belonged, was determined to defend it, and ensured that it remained a highly efficient force.

He handed over at the end of August 1963, whereupon he moved to Paris to take over as Deputy Supreme Allied Commander Europe under General Lemnitzer. His previous experience of working in NATO did not make him particularly enthusiastic about this appointment, and despite assurances that there really was a worthwhile job to do his doubts were confirmed. This was essentially a political appointment, lacking specific responsibilities, and he could do little beyond keeping an eye on what was happening. Nevertheless, as he put it, this was a nice way to leave the Service, which he did in March 1967. He retired to Harlow, where he devoted much time to activities in the nearby community, most notably local history and the organising of courses for young apprentices – a reflection perhaps of his earlier training as an engineer. He also retained his interest in the RAF, and is particularly well remembered by the Royal Air Forces Association, which he served as a much respected President from 1969-1978. He died in 1983.

To some Sir Thomas Pike seemed a somewhat remote, austere man. But for those who knew him well he was a sensitive, delightful companion. He had proved himself during his short period on active war operations as a most skilled and determined aviator; he had demonstrated great professional skills, including deep knowledge of the technical side of flying, in a number of key appointments; and as CAS he had stood up for his Service in an interminable series of most difficult debates. There remained further major battles to be fought before the shape of the RAF we know today could emerge, but he had preserved the essential fabric on which others would build.

Marshal of the Royal Air Force
The Lord Elworthy

The era from 1964 to 1970, which witnessed one of the most fundamental re-orientations of British defence policy since World War II, is widely referred to as the Healey Years, since it was Denis Healey, Secretary of State for Defence for the entire life-time of the Wilson Government, who oversaw the whole process. Less often remarked is the fact that Sir Charles Elworthy, first as Chief of the Air Staff and then as Chief of the Defence Staff, worked alongside him throughout; indeed he spent altogether eight years in these two appointments, exercising immense influence on the changing shape of both the Royal Air Force and the British Services as a whole.

Sam Elworthy, as he was always known to his contemporaries, was born in New Zealand in 1911, came to England in 1924 to attend Marlborough College, read Law at Trinity College Cambridge, and was then called to the Bar. Although he had not joined the University Air Squadron, preferring to devote his spare time to rowing, he already had an interest in aviation and decided on leaving Cambridge in 1933 to join the Reserve of Air Force Officers in order to fly. Two years later, having spent nine months in the Auxiliary Air Force flying the Hawker Hart as a member of 600 Squadron, he decided to make the RAF his career and took a permanent commission. His first posting was directly to 15 Squadron at Abingdon, where for two years he flew the Hart and then the Hind, and took part in the RAF's dive-bombing trials.

The end of 1937 brought Elworthy his first taste of higher politics when he became ADC to Sir Edgar Ludlow-Hewitt, CinC Bomber Command. He was thus in a position to observe the strengths and weaknesses of one of the RAF's most able commanders, to appreciate the enormous problems facing the bomber force with the approach of war, and to gain an inside view of the events of the time, notably the Munich crisis. On leaving Uxbridge in January 1939 he moved to Bassingbourn to join 108 Squadron, which had recently been re-equipped with the Blenheim, and on the outbreak of war the two squadrons there were switched to the training role and transferred to Bicester, where they later became 13 OTU with him as Chief Flying Instructor. Although disappointed not to be allowed an operational role, he had seen enough of the consequences of faulty flying technique to realise the need for better instruction, and his success in developing new procedures for night flying training led to the award of the Air Force Cross.

It was not until 26 August 1940 that he joined the front line by being posted to 82 Squadron at Watton. His new squadron had twice been virtually wiped out, over Gembloux on 17 May and Aalborg on 13 August, yet although he remained with it for only nine months, the last five months as its CO, it was when he departed one of the best squadrons in the RAF. Among other things he had bombed invasion barges, attempted to attack targets such as the

51 Sir Charles Elworthy, playing golf for the Air Force Board team against the British Aircraft Corporation at Wentworth, watches his partner, Air Chief Marshal Sir 'Gus' Walker, tee off using his one-arm swing, August 1963.

52 And afterwards there is time for a chat with Lord Portal.

53 *In 1964 the Air Council held one of its last meetings before being converted into the Air Force Board of the Defence Council. Left to right: Air Chief Marshal Sir Wallace Kyle (VCAS), Air Chief Marshal Sir Charles Elworthy (CAS), Rt Hon Hugh Fraser (Secretary-of-State for Air), Mr Julian Ridsdale (Parliamentary Under-Secretary of State), Mr J D Bryars (Private Secretary to S of S), Mr J Roberts, Air Marshal Sir John Davis (AMSO), Mr Martin Flett (PUS), Air Chief Marshal Sir Walter Cheshire (AMP), Air Marshal Sir Christopher Hartley (DCAS).*

54 *Sir Charles Elworthy, visiting Aden in 1966, in serious conversation with Air Vice-Marshal Humphrey, the AOC.*

55 *Sir Charles Elworthy on a visit to Hindustan Aeronautics Ltd at Bangalore, 1966.*

56 Two subsequent CASs are among RAF officers attending the Air Commanders' Conference at Headquarters Air South, Naples, in October 1962: Air Marshal Sir John Grandy (2nd row, third from left) and Air Vice-Marshal Spotswood (back row, second from left). Air Marshal The Earl of Bandon is on the front row (third from left), Air Marshal Sir Maurice Heath on Grandy's left, and Air Vice-Marshal Davis on the third row (second from right).

57 Sir John Grandy at Wittering to fly the Harrier.

58 *Sir John Grandy leaving Westminster Abbey after the laying of the Memorial Stone to Lord Dowding.*

59 Pilot Officer Spotswood (fourth from left) at Calshot, 1936.

60 Sir Denis Spotswood lecturing at the Indonesian Staff College.

61 Sir Denis Spotswood at Cranwell, 1971, after presenting the Prince of Wales with his "Wings".

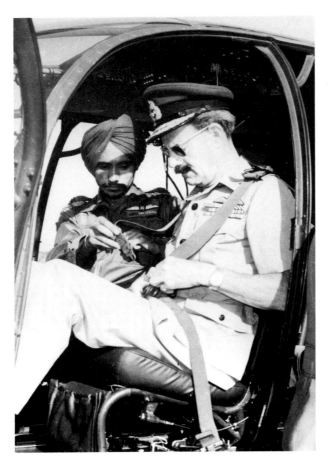

62 Sir Denis Spotswood on a visit to India, 1973.

63 And laying a wreath on Ghandi's tomb.

64 Wing Commander Humphrey after his record-breaking flight from Cape Town in ARIES IV, December 1953.

65 Sir Andrew Humphrey, as CinC Strike Command, takes part in an Air Sea Rescue exercise, 1971.

66 Sir Andrew Humphrey welcomes Admiral of the Fleet Sir Peter Hill-Norton, Chief of the Defence Staff, to Headquarters Strike Command, October 1971.

67 Sir Andrew Humphrey visits Air Marshal Sir Michael Beetham, CinC RAF Germany.

Dortmund-Ems Canal, and taken part in anti-shipping strikes, in one of which he hit an enemy tanker; as his DSO citation stated, "by his magnificent leadership and a complete disregard of danger, he brought his squadron to the highest peak of war efficiency".

Now an experienced bomber man, he was sent in May 1941 to work first in the Operations Room at Headquarters 2 Group and then at Headquarters Bomber Command, and a year later – soon after the arrival of Sir Arthur Harris – he became Group Captain Operations. He was thus closely involved in the affairs of Bomber Command throughout the period when the rationale of the bomber offensive was being questioned, the new techniques developed and the first great successes achieved. His daily routine became almost invariable, with advice from the intelligence and meteorological staffs, consideration of the current directive, the CinC's decision on the target, and the planning of the next attack, and he saw much of Harris himself. By April 1943, with the bomber offensive now at its height, he was ready to return to the front line and was chosen to command Waddington, one of the RAF's oldest stations and the home of 9, 44 and 50 Squadrons, all equipped with the Lancaster. Although the airfield had to be closed for a time while concrete runways were built, his squadrons continued to operate from the satellite airfields, and in November when Waddington itself re-opened two Australian squadrons, 463 and 467, moved in. At the same time a Base Headquarters was superimposed, an arrangement which Elworthy considered unnecessary. Well known attacks in which his squadrons played their part included those against Hamburg, Peenemunde, Berlin and – just before his departure – Nuremberg.

His next task, again at the instance of Harris, was to serve as his representative with the Headquarters of the Supreme Commander, General Eisenhower. With Bomber Command now committed to the direct support of Operation Overlord, there had to be close contact with Tedder, Leigh-Mallory and their staffs so as to ensure that the heavy bomber operations were properly integrated, and Elworthy played a key role. He was particularly involved in the detailed preparation of the Transportation Plan whereby it was hoped to cut the German rail communications without causing heavy French civilian casualties. Having thus for the first time experienced something of the political dimension in RAF planning, he was next offered the post of SASO at Headquarters 5 Group, under Ralph Cochrane, and he remained there for the rest of the war, overseeing a whole series of specialised operations including the sinking of the Tirpitz.

Incredible as it may seem to us today, he had by May 1945 held the rank of Air Commodore for almost a year, yet was still aged only 34, and had never served outside Bomber Command. Reverting now to lower rank he was retained yet again in the bomber role, being sent to the Central Bombing Establishment at Marham to start developing tactics for the first of the new generation of jet bombers, the Canberra. At the beginning of 1947, however, his career pattern changed when he went to India as SASO of 2 (Indian) Group and then, after Independence, was seconded to the new Pakistan Air Force where he commanded their base at Drigh Road and doubled as Air Force Member of the Defence Council. Returning home in 1949 and realising that his total lack of formal staff training threatened to restrict his advancement in the Service, he persuaded the Air Member for Personnel to let him attend the Joint

Services Staff College at Latimer, albeit initially as a Wing Commander.

Almost inevitably the Air Ministry now beckoned, but instead of the Air Staff post that he might have hoped for he was appointed a Deputy Director of Personnel, concerned with officers' postings; he thought it "the kiss of death" but subsequently realised just how valuable had been this experience of personnel administration. It was his outspokenness there about Fighter Command's refusal to employ senior officers without a fighter background which led to his own next appointment to command Tangmere, his first operational post outside Bomber Command. Two Meteor day-fighter squadrons, 1 and 29, were based there and Elworthy took every opportunity to fly with them. He departed in March 1953 for another Meteor station, Odiham, having been specially chosen to take over for the period leading up to the Queen's Coronation Review in July. The detailed planning, preparations and aftermath of this event kept him fully occupied until the end of the year when he became Commander of Fighter Command's Metropolitan Sector at North Weald. He spent two years there, concerned with the protection of South-East England against possible Soviet air attack, before going to the Imperial Defence College in 1956.

Here, as with a number of other officers, his studies were interrupted in August by the Suez emergency, when he was selected as the Chief of Denis Barnett's Planning Staff, but within days – having already become immersed in, and frustrated by, the political complexities – he was taken ill and rushed to hospital. The doctors worked well and by the end of the year he was fit enough to start his 2½ year appointment as Commandant of the Staff College at Bracknell. He found this an enjoyable time, and it provided much opportunity to broaden his own horizons and bring himself up-to-date on the major issues of RAF policy arising from the Sandys Defence Review. Consequently he was well placed to join the Air Council in November 1959 as Deputy Chief of Air Staff, responsible for training, operational requirements and signals. Yet he had hardly had time to find his feet than he was on his way again, at the specific instance of Lord Mountbatten, Chief of the Defence Staff, to become Commander-in-Chief of the first post-war integrated command, British Forces Aden Peninsula, soon to be re-titled Middle East Command.

In setting up this new organisation in the face of considerable single-Service resistance he was firmly backed by Mountbatten and in due course a remarkable degree of co-operation was achieved between the three Services and the civil administration. This paid off in July 1961, when the carefully prepared plan Vantage was put into effect in order to protect Kuwait against the threat of an Iraqi attack. This was a major joint operation, and Elworthy takes a share of the credit for its success. By the time he departed in 1963 the unified command had been severely tested, both operationally and administratively, and in its efficiency gave proof of Elworthy's talents for achieving harmony between the three Services and handling the political intricacies. These qualities augured well for both his remaining Service appointments.

He became Chief of the Air Staff in September 1963, hoping to encounter the same inter-Service harmony as he had experienced in Aden, but was quickly disappointed, and controversy raged for most of his time in Whitehall. His service there largely coincided with that of Denis Healey as Secretary of State, a man with whom he generally got along well and who – unlike the other

Chiefs of Staff, in Lord Cameron's view* – did not overshadow him. Even before Healey's arrival on the scene there had been disagreements with the Navy over aircraft purchases, but soon after the advent of the Labour Government in 1964 a much bigger question came to a head: the future of the TSR2, a project Elworthy had already been involved with as DCAS. With costs escalating rapidly, the numbers to be purchased being steadily cut, and the only prospective overseas purchasers – the Australians – deciding against, Elworthy accepted its cancellation, given the Government's intention to order the F111 instead. The HS681 also, which he saw as over-ambitious and almost extravagant, was dropped in favour of the C130, a good buy for the RAF, thus marking the end of the peacetime policy of always buying British military aircraft. The one major British project that did survive was the P1127 Harrier, which was ordered after the abandonment of the supersonic P1154 and became an important part of the RAF's front line.

Another major pre-occupation was Britain's world-wide role, especially East of Suez. The Confrontation with Indonesia demanded considerable attention and Elworthy visited the Far East several times, not least in order to defend the RAF in face of unfair Army criticism of the performance of its helicopter squadrons. Moreover these operations provided a constant reminder of the extent to which all three Services were now stretched and much time was spent considering how far such commitments should be retained and by what means. Among these issues was the carrier controversy which led to the First Sea Lord's resignation in 1966; Elworthy was not opposed to large carriers per se, but since he thought it no longer practicable to provide sufficient of them, he believed the job must be done in different ways. Other issues were the evacuation from Aden and the possibility of military intervention in Rhodesia, which he strongly opposed and was the only matter on which he might ever have considered resigning. More domestic concerns included the withdrawal of the Valiant, the planned re-organisation of the RAF's home command structure, and the decision to end the cadet entry at Cranwell, which he thought essential in the light of changing national patterns of education.

His period as CAS ended in April 1967, and four months later he took over as Chief of the Defence Staff. Having been favoured for the post by Mountbatten and having worked under both him and Richard Hull, he was very much the heir apparent, and over the next four years he exercised much influence on defence policy under both Denis Healey and later Lord Carrington. This was in his view a period of great and alarming Soviet expansion, marked particularly by the Czech crisis of 1968, and he accompanied Healey to many of the NATO meetings where the new policy of flexible response was already being developed. Several times he visited Northern Ireland, where the emergency had just begun causing severe problems, particularly for the Army and its garrison in Germany. He was bitterly disappointed, too, at the cancellation of the F111 against the advice of the Air Staff. On a more constructive note, the deterrent role was successfully transferred from the V Force to the Polaris submarines, planning was started for the multi-role combat aircraft, the military salary was introduced, and the position of CDS was

* See page 82

gradually strengthened. By the time he departed in April 1971 the main withdrawal from the Far East was virtually complete, and United Kingdom defence policy was firmly set towards concentration on the support of NATO in Europe and the North Atlantic. Soon afterwards he was created a Life Peer, the first RAF officer to be awarded a peerage since the high wartime Commanders.

He spent the next seven years as Constable and Governor of Windsor Castle, and for most of the time also as Lord Lieutenant of Greater London; in addition he held several business and academic appointments. Then in 1978 he decided to return to his native New Zealand where he has lived ever since, returning to England usually once a year, his visits generally timed to enable him to attend the Garter Ceremony and perform his duties as a Steward at Henley Royal Regatta. The Royal Air Force recalls him as one of its most distinguished Chiefs of Staff. Very much a bomber man he had never been a single-Service Commander-in-Chief and had served only briefly on the Air Staff in Whitehall, yet as both CAS and CDS he was held in the highest regard by Service colleagues and politicians alike during the years when the United Kingdom finally came to terms with the fact that she was no longer a world power.

Marshal of the Royal Air Force
Sir John Grandy

One of the greatest distinctions that any RAF officer can claim is to have fought in the Battle of Britain, and particularly as a squadron commander. Yet only one Chief of the Air Staff can claim that special accolade: Sir John Grandy, who led 249 Squadron in the summer of 1940.

John Grandy was born in Northwood in 1913 and during his schooldays, when he attended University College School, he spent much of his spare time watching the flying at Northolt and soon decided that this was the career he wanted. Having overcome his parents' initial misgivings, he joined the RAF on a Short Service Commission in September 1931 and within a year, having been taught to fly at 5 Flying Training School at Sealand, he had joined his first operational squadron. Fifty four Squadron, which had had a distinguished record in the First World War, had recently been re-formed at Hornchurch, equipped with the Bulldog, and Grandy spent three fairly carefree years with it. His abiding impressions of this formative period were the importance of the squadron, the key role of the commanding officer, and not least the value of having his own aircraft fitter.

His first move came in April 1935 when he went as an instructor to 604 (County of Middlesex) Squadron at Hendon, where the Wapiti was being replaced by the Hart and the Demon, several of which then took part in the Royal Review at Mildenhall. The following year 604 was awarded the Esher Trophy for the most efficient Auxiliary Air Force squadron, and Grandy recalls with gratitude his brief opportunity to work with the Auxiliaries, which did so much to bring the RAF into contact with the public in the pre-war years. He left 604 Squadron early in 1936 to undergo the flying instructors' course at the Central Flying School, and having been awarded a permanent commission was for the next four years employed almost continuously on instructional duties, some of the time at 9 and 13 Flying Training Schools (at Thornaby and Drem respectively), but mainly with the London University Air Squadron. A projected overseas posting in 1938 having failed to materialise, Grandy – now an A1 Instructor – continued to play his part in the urgent expansion of flying training in these critical years, and feels that despite the many pressures standards were well maintained.

When war broke out he was still at 13 FTS, and not until April 1940, after a few months at the Central Gunnery School, was he allowed to join in the action. His initial task was to succeed Richard Atcherley in command of 219 Squadron, equipped with Blenheim fighters, at Catterick, and he stayed there only a month, carrying out routine night patrols over North East England. Having quickly expressed to the AOC, Air Vice-Marshal Saul, his views on the unsuitability of the Blenheim for this role, he was sent to take command of the re-formed 249 Squadron at Church Fenton on 16 May. With the Battle of

France now under way Fighter Command needed every squadron it could get, and Grandy was ordered to bring 249 to war standard as quicky as possible. He and his men, none of whom had previous operational experience, immediately started intensive training on the Spitfire at Leconfield, and despite having to switch to the Hurricane in June the squadron was in action on 8 July and declared fully operational at Church Fenton the next day.

Five weeks later, with the Battle of Britain approaching its peak, 249 was moved to Boscombe Down and into the main action; within two days one of its pilots, Flying Officer Nicolson, fought the engagement for which he would receive the Victoria Cross, the only one to be awarded in the Battle of Britain. Then on 1 September, Grandy took his squadron to North Weald, where it remained for the rest of the Battle, heavily engaged throughout and eventually being credited with destroying more German aircraft than any other. To his intense annoyance he himself missed part of the action, being shot down by an Me 109 on 6 September and having to spend some time in hospital, but he saw enough to feel the excitement and the fear, to remember the quality of the leadership – notably that of Keith Park and Victor Beamish, his own commanding officer – and to realise that the Germans had lost through faulty tactics.

On leaving the squadron in December 1940 he worked briefly for Sholto Douglas in the Operations Room at Fighter Command before spending a year first at 52 Operational Training Unit and then at Coltishall. His next move was to Duxford, where he took command in February 1942 in order to run the first Typhoon Wing. Intended as the successor to the Hurricane, the Typhoon was presenting serious engine and other problems, and to restore morale and get the aircraft operational was a major test of leadership. Having flown on the Wing's first operational sweep and observed the Typhoon's performance in the Dieppe Raid in August, he was soon aware of its limitations as an interceptor; it had obvious potential, however, for low-level strike and its later outstanding success in both the ground and anti-shipping roles owed much to the perseverance of Grandy and his colleagues in the early days at Duxford. He recalls being particularly well served by industry; by his administrators, most of whom were much older; and by the WAAF, whose arrival on his station he had originally opposed.

February 1943 saw him on his way again, this time to North Africa, where he was placed in command of 210 Air Defence Group, charged with the air defence of the recently captured port of Tripoli, through which many of the supplies for the Tunisian campaign would have to flow. A combination of Beaufighters, Spitfires, Hurricanes and anti-aircraft guns proved sufficient to deal with the enemy attacks, and as the Mediterranean battles moved away the threat diminished. Consequently by September 1943 there was relatively little to do in Tripolitania and he was sent to the Canal Zone to command 73 (Fighter) Operational Training Unit, based first at Abu Sueir and then at Fayid. Important though such work was and pleasant as the life style might be, this was a frustrating period for a young Group Captain who longed to be at the scene of the action and felt the war was passing him by, and having had no success in his attempts to talk his way back to fighters or into the Yugoslav air supply operations, he had to soldier on in the Middle East until the end of 1944.

Ideally he would now have liked to be in on the climax of the European war, but instead he was posted to the Far East to run 341 Wing, comprising four Dakota squadrons, for the last seven months of the Japanese War. By now there was little air opposition and the main problems encountered in his squadrons' multifarious air transport operations arose from the appalling weather and poor maps. The leadership provided by men such as Mountbatten, Slim and Bandon he recalls as inspiring, and he was much impressed by the mutual respect existing between the Army and the RAF who were working so closely together. Even so the invasion of Malaya planned for September would in his opinion have been very difficult and he was thankful that the atomic bomb rendered it unnecessary. He remained in Singapore as SASO at Headquarters 232 Group until the beginning of 1946, much involved in such matters as the repatriation of prisoners-of-war and the campaign in the Netherlands East Indies.

On returning home he went first as a student to the Army Staff College, where he fought the war all over again, and then to the Air Ministry to work for Basil Embry on operational training, remaining until 1949. Like others he found this a frustrating period filled with doubts and questions about the future, but the chance to fly the Mosquito twice to Singapore helped relieve the gloom, and the two-year spell as Air Attache in Brussels that followed proved of great interest and provided valuable insights into the diplomatic scene and the beginnings of Western European Union. The end of 1950 saw him back at last in Fighter Command, where he felt he belonged, and over the next six years he served first at Headquarters Northern Sector, next at Bentley Priory, and finally as Commandant of the Central Fighter Establishment. With the Command still organised broadly on wartime lines and the manned bomber threat still paramount, there was little awareness of the vast changes to come, and the main problems facing Grandy and his colleagues were the obsolescence of the first generation of jet fighters and the introduction of the second, notably the Hunter and the Javelin, with both of which he was much concerned.

So far John Grandy's career could be called fairly predictable, and he was greatly surprised, having completed only part of the 1957 course at the Imperial Defence College, to be appointed to command the second phase of Operation Grapple, the United Kingdom hydrogen bomb tests at Christmas Island. The memorable year that followed was marked for him by an impressive degree of inter-service and scientific collaboration; he recalls insisting on the meticulous observance of the laid-down safety precautions, and finding the actual tests both impresssive and sobering. While he had no doubts about the importance of the tests, the experience convinced him that the existence of weapons of such power now made major war virtually unthinkable.

By the end of 1958 he was back in the Air Ministry, this time as ACAS (Ops); while there were many policy changes under way arising from the Sandys Defence Review, Grandy's work was mainly concerned with current operations and served as a good lead-in for the three successive Commander-in-Chief appointments that lay ahead. The first of these was in Germany, where the building of the Berlin Wall in 1961, soon after his arrival, did nothing to decrease the tension between East and West. Yet he had to cope – reluctantly – with major reductions in the number of squadrons and their concentration mainly on the clutch airfields West of the Rhine. At the same time much attention had to be devoted to helping to integrate the Belgian,

Dutch and West German Air Forces into 2nd ATAF, and to fostering co-operation with BAOR, for whom he realised that the RAF was doing too little in the close support rules.

From Germany he went in 1963 to Bomber Command, taking over its highly efficient force from Sir Kenneth Cross. By now, Skybolt having been cancelled and Polaris ordered, the V Force was needing to switch to low-level operations owing to its increasing vulnerability, and Grandy had not just to grasp a hitherto unfamiliar aspect of air power but to adapt it to a new concept. He also had to cope with the withdrawal of the Valiant squadrons through metal fatigue, and to inform SACEUR (General Lemnitzer) that they were no longer available; nevertheless Bomber Command remained highly effective in the deterrent role, and when Tom Pike told Grandy that he would next go to the Far East he advised him that his appointment as CAS might follow.

When John Grandy arrived in Singapore in May 1965 the Confrontation with Indonesia was still in progress, and as C in C of the unified command he had responsibility for a campaign involving not just the three British Services but also the forces of several Commonwealth countries. It thus provided invaluable experience of co-ordinating joint military operations and of high level politics – he dealt with no fewer than five Prime Ministers; he was also able to observe at fairly close quarters the difficulties being encountered by the Americans in Vietnam. By the time he returned home at the beginning of 1967 to become CAS he had not only witnessed the successful conclusion of Confrontation but gained almost unparalleled knowledge of the RAF front line. If it was something of a disadvantage to have never served on the Air Council or, as it was now, the Air Force Board, in all other respects he was thoroughly qualified for his new appointment.

Having taken over on 1 April 1967 John Grandy found himself in the unusual situation of working under an officer of his own Service, Sir Charles Elworthy, as Chief of the Defence Staff, but fortunately, given the personalities of the two men, this presented no problems. Nor at that time were there any great difficulties with the leaders of the other Services: all were being urged to economise and to agree to further strengthening of the Central Staff, and none was enthusiastic at the prospect, though admittedly the Ministry itself was too big. Grandy, although a firm believer in the three Services being separate professions whose identity must be preserved, also saw it as essential to understand the views of his Army and Navy colleagues, and did much to try to heal the wounds that had been caused by the dispute over the Navy's large carriers. Realising how hard it was for them to accept their change of role, he set much store by encouraging the Fleet Air Arm to co-operate closely with the RAF.

Much happened during his four years as CAS, including all the closing stages of the main British withdrawals from the Persian Gulf and the Far East, events whose inevitability for reasons of economy he accepted with the greatest reluctance. The cancellation of the proposed Anglo-French Variable Geometry aircraft and of the order for the F111 entailed a major rearrangement of the future aircraft requirement and complex discussion with Denis Healey, with whom he worked for most of his time in office. There was a tinge of sadness too in July 1969, when he sent a signal to mark the transfer of the strategic nuclear deterrent role to the Royal Navy, but as he observed: "the task has meant maintaining, at all times through seven years, the highest state of readiness which the RAF has known in peacetime". On the more positive side one of the RAF's great success stories, the Harrier, entered squadron service in that same year, and even more important the decision was taken – jointly with West Germany and Italy – to develop the multi-role combat aircraft, eventually to be known as the Tornado. Moreover, the establishment of Strike Command in face of strong emotional resistance from the traditionalists paved the way for the United Kingdom command structure that we know today. When he handed over in April 1971 his was an Air Force that had been much changed under the pressures of economy, but was still intact.

Since then he has filled two major appointments: from 1973 to 1978 he served as Governor and Commander-in-Chief of Gibraltar, the first RAF officer to occupy this post, and he spent the next ten years as Constable and Governor of Windsor Castle. In addition he has been involved with many charitable committees, both Service and civilian, and was until recently Chairman of the Trustees of the Imperial War Museum, where he continued to demonstrate his fundamental belief in the importance of close ties between all three Services.

Marshal of the Royal Air Force
Sir Denis Spotswood

When one recalls that the Royal Air Force was derived in part from the Royal Naval Air Service and considers that the maritime role has always been of prime importance, it seems surprising that only one or two of its Chiefs of Staff have been drawn from that particular background. Sir Denis Spotswood, who spent his pre-war years and much of World War II in maritime operations, is one of that small group.

A Londoner born in 1916, Denis Spotswood was educated at Kingston Grammar School and in 1932 joined the Evening Standard with a view to making his career in journalism. Three years later, however, when he was rowing with Alan Scarf, later to be posthumously awarded the VC for his bravery in the face of the Japanese invasion of Malaya, the two of them decided to join the RAF; since he was now too old to try for a Cranwell cadetship he entered the Service on a Short Service Commission in March 1936. Within two months he had completed 50 hours' flying instruction on the Miles Hawk at the Reading civil flying school, and in August, a mere four months after arriving at 6 Flying Training School at Netheravon, was awarded his Wings. He left Netheravon in January 1937, having been selected for the 'general reconnaissance' role, and moved to Bircham Newton to convert to the Anson prior to attending a specialist navigation course.

By now, however, he had set his heart on flying boats, and July saw him at Calshot learning to fly the Southampton and the Scapa, whereupon he joined 201 Squadron and was shortly detached to Felixstowe to work in collaboration with Watson-Watt on the development of Radio Direction Finding. Finding Felixstowe to his liking, he subsequently contrived a posting to 209 Squadron, which was equipped with the Singapore, soon to be replaced by the Stranraer, and a year later by the Lerwick. To add to the variety Spotswood himself had some interesting detachments, one of them to the Shetlands, which resulted in the selection of Sullom Voe as a war base, and the other to the Far East, flying the RAF's second Sunderland. He remained with 209 – now at Invergordon – when the war started, moving to a variety of bases including Oban, Pembroke Dock, Stranraer and Lough Erne, from which the Lerwicks carried out the tedious and largely routine patrolling of the Western approaches that was the lot of Coastal Command in those early days. The aircraft itself was not in his view as bad as some of its critics have alleged, but the equipment was poor and there were many disappointments. In April 1941, however, the squadron was re-equipped with the Catalina and on 15 May his luck changed when he sighted and attacked a U-boat, which he was subsequently credited with damaging. A few days later it was Spotswood's aircraft, being flown by his second pilot Pilot Officer Briggs, since he had 'flu, that found the German battleship Bismarck. He finally left 209 in August, after two years of operational flying which, though unspectacular, had taught him much – and not least about self-reliance and man-management.

His next task, instructing at the Hudson Operational Training Unit, arose almost fortuitously since he had been sent to Canada to collect a Catalina and instead returned flying a Hudson because there was no Catalina available, whereupon he was chosen to teach others to fly it. He did this for six months and was then personally instructed by Sir Philip Joubert, CinC Coastal Command, to take command of 500 Squadron, which was in poor state. Soon afterwards the squadron was moved from Stornaway to St Eval, where it took part in anti-U-Boat operations over the Bay of Biscay before being sent to Gibraltar in November 1942 to take part in Operation Torch, the invasion of North Africa. Within days of the landings, 500 found themselves first at Tafaroui and then Blida, near Algiers, a virtually bare base where they had to support themselves and live by improvisation – invaluable experience as Spotswood recalls, and made all the better by their success in sinking at least four of the 22 U-boats they attacked during their four-month stay.

On returning home in April 1943, Spotswood was told that his extensive maritime experience was needed in the Air Ministry's Directorate of Air Tactics, where he spent four months before attending the short No 10 War Staff Course at Bulstrode, learning the practicalities of staff work and extending his knowledge of other types of air operations. Hoping now, as an Acting Group Captain, to be given command of a station, he was instead sent to the Far East to join the small Anglo-American planning team which worked for Mountbatten first in Delhi and then in Ceylon. To begin with the team was in the unsatisfactory situation of being isolated from the main staffs, but once the Supreme Allied Commander had been persuaded to rectify matters the organisation worked well and Spotswood, who had great admiration for the way in which Mountbatten raised the morale of his Command, accompanied him on a number of his tours. He thus had an excellent opportunity to get to know many of the high commanders, and to learn at first-hand just how essential air power was to the winning of the Far Eastern war. Once it was over he remained in Singapore for a few months, mainly engaged in planning the recovery of the Allied prisoners-of-war and internees, before returning to England at the end of 1945.

Having had no doubts about accepting the permanent commission that was on offer he now spent two years on the Directing Staff at the RAF Staff College, where the main task was to re-orientate their war experienced students to the needs of peacetime, before moving to what was for him a new sphere: night fighters. Coltishall, which he commanded throughout 1948 and 1949, had three squadrons of Mosquitos (23, 141 and 264) which were being built up to higher states of readiness in face of the growing Soviet threat, and despite the problems posed by the rapid turn-around of national service ground tradesmen he enjoyed his time there, taking every opportunity to fly the aircraft himself. After this it was back once again to staff training but this time as Junior Directing Staff at the Imperial Defence College, where he met many of those who would hold the most senior positions in their Services in the years to come.

His experience was now to be further extended when, having completed a jet conversion course, he went on an exchange posting to the USA as Deputy

Chief of the Tactical Operations Plans Branch at USAF Headquarters in the Pentagon. As one of the early RAF officers to hold such an appointment he found the Americans initially somewhat reluctant to accept him, but he was soon fully integrated into the planning team for USAF operations in North-West Europe; he was also involved in developing the Caribbean missile range. These two years in Washington proved invaluable for the knowledge of American attitudes and methods, and for the friendships established.

In the summer of 1954 Spotswood was home again, surprised and pleased – thanks to the personal intervention of Sir William Dickson – to be allowed a second tour in command of a fighter station. This time it was Linton-on-Ouse, the home of 66 and 92 Squadrons (the only squadrons outside Germany to be equipped with the F86 Sabre), a Meteor night fighter squadron, No 264, and a helicopter ASR flight. Altogether Linton had more than 70 aircraft, and what with the changeover to centralised servicing – unavoidable in view of the dearth of technical expertise – and the arrival of the Hunter in early 1956 there was plenty to keep him occupied. The conversion to the Hunter was particularly interesting, since there were no two-seater aircraft, and the engine stopped when the guns were fired!

Towards the end of 1956 his attention was turned from such practical matters to the realms of higher policy when he joined Sir Dermot Boyle's staff as Deputy Director of Plans, just in time for all the turmoil that arose from the Sandys Defence Review. Much of his time was spent working with his Navy and Army opposite numbers, but while he fully supported the joint planning system he had great misgivings about Mountbatten's campaign for a much stronger "Centre". He left the Ministry in mid-1958 with some relief, mixed with surprise and delight at being appointed Commandant of the RAF College – surprise since he had not been a Flight Cadet himself, and delight in view of the special challenge. A firm believer in the traditional Cranwell system and its central role in the officer structure, he was convinced of the need to raise entry standards, to provide the opportunity for cadets to read for an external degree at the College, and to bring the Technical Cadets from Henlow to Cranwell so that all young permanent officers would train together. All three changes, together with the necessary new buildings, were firmly in hand by the time he left in early 1961, and while he was later very disappointed that his pattern of training proved so short-lived, he was delighted to see so many Flight Cadets of his time reaching high rank.

Spotswood's next move was to SHAPE, where his experiences of air defence and working with the Americans were brought together as Assistant Chief of Staff in the Air Defence Division. As well as dealing with many day-to-day matters he was responsible for developing a system whereby the various NATO control systems could be electronically co-ordinated, and for negotiating on behalf of General Norstad an air defence agreement with the French. He stayed at SHAPE until October 1963, learning much about the international scene, and then spent a very important few months chairing the Pathfinder Study into the future shape, size and cost of the RAF front line. Many of the recommendations of his wide-ranging report, which also urged a more flexible procurement policy, were accepted, including that which led to the creation of Strike Command four years later.

So far his operational experience had been confined to maritime and fighter aircraft, but in July 1964, after a couple of conversion courses, he became AOC 3 Group, responsible for Bomber Command's Valiant and Victor squadrons, and for air-to-air refuelling. There was more than enough to do in running the Group, particularly with the switch to low-level operations, and he was unlucky enough to have to cope with the grounding of the Valiant force in 1965 owing to metal fatigue, but by the end of that year he was ready for his first top-level appointment, Commander in Chief of RAF Germany and Commander 2nd Allied Tactical Air Force. 1967 and 1968 were particularly difficult years in Germany, with the sheer scale of the Soviet threat the ever-present anxiety but now coupled with pressure for further economies, which would include the concentration of his limited number of ageing aircraft on even fewer highly vulnerable airfields. In the longer term the situation would improve, but at this stage Spotswood could only try to prevent the infrastructure being eroded too far and preserve the RAF's influence with the Americans and the other NATO air forces, and of course BAOR. He was indeed fortunate in knowing his way around the system from his previous years at SHAPE.

His second high-level appointment came in August 1968 when he was sent to run the recently formed Strike Command that he himself had proposed. He well understood the suspicion of the fighter and bomber lobbies at being forced into one organisation, and the even greater reluctance of the men of Coastal Command to join in a year later. But in his view the cost of modern aircraft, together with the smaller numbers that would be available in future and their ubiquity, necessitated their flexible employment and therefore centralised control; the Groups would retain their specialised expertise but Strike Command would tell them what to do. So for nearly three years he oversaw the development of the new concept, seeking to sell it to all who needed persuading, including the Navy, and overcoming the inevitable series of administrative problems; at the same time the overseas withdrawals were giving Strike Command extra responsibilities and a whole series of new aircraft and ground installations were coming into service. He was thus thoroughly conversant with the present-day Air Force when he was appointed to succeed John Grandy in April 1971.

Sir Denis Spotswood's three years as CAS could be seen in some ways as a period of consolidation after the many changes of the late 1960s, the "Healey years". A new generation of aircraft had been introduced following on the many cancellations, the overseas withdrawals were almost complete, the RAF structure had been reorganised; what was now needed was the chance to draw breath and adjust to the new situation in which Britain's main defence effort was to be centred on the NATO area. Yet the pressures continued under the Heath government, notably for even more savings, and in urging the need for further RAF economies – unpopular in many quarters – Spotswood felt that otherwise the very continuance of the Third Service might be at risk. At the same time he had a lot to do in ensuring that the new aircraft, notably the Phantom, Harrier, Buccaneer, Nimrod and Hercules, were being properly used, and in negotiating with the West Germans and Italians over the MRCA; each nation needed the aircraft, each had to retain its own industrial base, and he recognised that everyone must be prepared to compromise if the project was to succeed. There was also an important change in the aircraft supply organisation, namely the incorporation of the Controllerate (Aircraft) within the new Procurement Executive; for him this was a sound move, and he was able to insist on the Controller of Aircraft continuing to be an RAF officer with a seat on the Air Force Board.

Not surprisingly one of his major concerns was to improve the NATO links: in securing for the RAF the ACOS Plans and Policy post at SHAPE, and negotiating for CinC Strike Command to become a Major Subordinate Commander under SACEUR, he ensured a fuller role for the RAF in NATO's forward thinking. He was less enthusiastic, however, about the attempt to reinstate a limited military presence in the Far East in the absence of anything in the Middle East, although he stipulated that the RAF must do all it could to support the new Five Power Defence Agreement.

If there was one field where he had felt himself ill-equipped as CAS it was in his limited knowledge of industry, but the deficiency was remedied as soon as he retired from the post in April 1974, for he was immediately appointed Vice-Chairman of Rolls Royce, a post he held for six years. The Presidency of SBAC and Directorships of the Dowty Group and Smith's Industries also came his way, and among his Service interests were the Chairmanship of the Trustees of the RAF Museum, in which he succeeded Sir Dermot Boyle, and of the Royal Star and Garter Home. Though now less involved in the business world he retains his close interest in the Royal Air Force in which he spent a wide-ranging and satisfying career.

Marshal of the Royal Air Force Sir Andrew Humphrey

Sir Andrew Humphrey, whose Service career was sadly cut short soon after reaching its peak, was a Chief whose great abilities as a leader and an advocate of air power were matched by superb skill as a pilot. Indeed one theme ran through all the tributes paid to him after his death: respect and admiration for a man who had not only the many qualities required of a CAS and CDS but had also displayed throughout his career the greatest talent as a professional airman – though incredibly he had never commanded a squadron.

Born in 1921 in Edinburgh he was educated at Bradfield College, and as a teenager who was thrilled by the stories of the air fighting in the First World War he decided early on to make the RAF his career and set his heart on a cadetship at Cranwell. He was just 18 when he entered the College in January 1939, and a mere 15 months later he had completed his training and received his permanent commission; to meet the urgent need for qualified pilots his course had been shortened and – having overcome some early problems with air sickness – he was ready for operational training. Instead, somewhat surprisingly, he was sent initially to 9 Bombing and Gunnery School in North Wales, where for four months he flew trainee bomb aimers and air gunners in the Hawker Demon. In September 1940, however, such was Fighter Command's need for more pilots at the height of the Battle of Britain that he was pulled out to undertake a ten-day Spitfire conversion course at Hawarden, and on the 16th he found himself joining 266 Squadron at Wittering.

266 Squadron was at that time operating in the Duxford Wing under the leadership of Douglas Bader, and on 28 September he flew his first operational sortie as part of it. Two months later, on 4 December, he shot down an He 111 which he had spotted over the Dutch coast, and as day patrols continued throughout the winter, supplemented in early 1941 by occasional sweeps over the French coast, his experience grew. In March, when his Spitfire crashed in flames owing to an engine fault, he was lucky to survive with only minor injuries. By now the German night bombers were posing the main threat, and unsuitable though the Spitfire was as a night fighter Humphrey and others were determined to have a go. Persistence was rewarded when on 8/9 May 1941, while patrolling near Derby, he destroyed his second Heinkel, and two nights later, having chased an enemy bomber to the Dutch coast, he shot it down and immediately destroyed another that had just taken off; the subsequent DFC citation spoke of "great keenness", an indication of the skill and determination he was already displaying.

Humphrey left 266 Squadron in July 1941, spent a month with the recently formed 452 Squadron at Kenley, when he shot down an Me 109, and then went to the Spitfire Operational Training Unit at Grangemouth as an instructor. The following March he was back on operations, this time as a Flight Commander with a newly formed Hurricane squadron, 175, based at Warmwell in Dorset. By now Hurricanes often carried bombs, and Humphrey was "annoyed beyond words" when he had to abort his very first mission against Maupertus airfield owing to an engine problem. He fared better later on, and on 9 May he obtained 175's first "kills" by shooting down two Me 109s from a formation of six that he had attacked. He had done much for the new squadron and was greatly missed when he returned to Grangemouth in June.

His considerable flying skills having now been amply demonstrated, he was selected in January 1943 to spend a few months at the specialised low attack instructors' school at Milfield, and for the rest of the war he remained in this role, working first in the Middle East and then the Far East. For the most part he flew Hurricanes or Beaufighters, and his six months with 6 Squadron in Tunisia and the Canal Zone from July 1943 onwards were fairly typical: "he trained pilots in the rocket projectile role, directed the assembling of the equipment and introduced many modifications to the armament". Having led the squadron in battle-formation exercises, amply demonstrated his own prowess as a marksman, and developed a close liaison with the Army, he must have been most disappointed when he was not allowed to accompany them to Italy in early 1944 and instead remained at Shallufa and later Nicosia as an instructor. Then in November he moved to Ranchi, in Bengal, to apply his skills in training Mosquito crews for the ground attack role in the Burma campaign – and in the process collecting a reprimand for negligently damaging an aircraft. He remained in India after the war, serving in New Delhi in the Secretariat of the Commander-in-Chief, Lord Auchinleck, before leaving for home in May 1946.

Two months later he reported to Headquarters 106 Group, shortly to become the Central Photographic Establishment, at RAF Benson, where he flew mainly Spitfires and Mosquitos and learnt the art of photographic reconnaissance. Such was his aptitude for this entirely new role that in late 1948 he was chosen to join 82 Squadron as one of its Flight Commanders. No 82 Squadron, equipped with seven Lancasters and two Dakotas, had been at Eastleigh, near Nairobi, since mid-1947 and was tasked to carry out the first aerial mapping survey of British Africa under the direction of the Colonial Office. This was a fascinating, varied and often very difficult task, given that it covered areas in many different parts of the continent, and often had to be undertaken in very hazardous weather conditions. It therefore called not just for great flying skills, but also for adaptability and much attention to the needs of the ground personnel, and in all respects Humphrey distinguished himself. He flew surveys in Transjordan, West Africa, Kenya, Tanganyika, and the Rhodesias, took part in flying displays, exercises with the Army and Navy, and demonstration flights to counter civil unrest, and also did much of the planning. Usually he flew one of the Lancasters – including PA 474, which still flies today with the Battle of Britain Memorial Flight – and on one occasion, in January 1951, nearly suffered a fatal accident. While crossing the Sahara with a replacement aircraft, his controls failed to respond when he tried to disengage the autopilot and at 10,000 feet the Lancaster went into an almost vertical dive; although he managed to pull out and eventually land safely the stresses had damaged the aircraft beyond repair.

Soon afterwards he was home again attending No 2 Course at the RAF

Flying College, Manby, a course designed to give practical training in flying and navigating in all-weather conditions, and at the end of 1951 he stayed on as Syndicate Leader and then Senior Instructor, which gave him the chance to take part in some of the special Aries flights. As a student he had flown as co-pilot with Wing Commander Bob Frogley over the North Pole in the Lincoln ARIES III; two years later, in December 1953, he piloted ARIES IV, a Canberra B2, on its record-breaking flight from Cape Town to London, and in 1954 – relying largely on astro-navigation – he flew the same aircraft on the first jet flight to the North Pole. Now widely recognised as an exceptionally talented pilot and instructor, he was an obvious selection for the Staff College course in 1955.

His next posting provided an ideal opportunity to use his flying experience in an Air Ministry appointment. First as a Wing Commander in the Operational Requirements Branch and then as a Deputy Director he had special responsibility for the development of the RAF's first supersonic fighter, the Lightning; he often flew it himself and played a leading part in developing its instrumentation and automatic flight control systems. Yet so far he had held no proper command appointment, and in February 1959 the omission was rectified when he was chosen to take charge of the RAF's newest major base, Akrotiri. His arrival in Cyprus coincided with the Lancaster House Agreement that marked the end of the EOKA campaign and led during his time to Cypriot independence and the establishment of the Sovereign Base Areas, and much of his attention was devoted to the further development of Akrotiri to meet this new situation. His four Canberra B6 squadrons and one PR7 squadron were another major preoccupation, not least since the strike aircraft were now being given a nuclear capability. Akrotiri was also an important staging and reinforcement airfield, whose facilities were demonstrated with particular success in the Kuwait operation of June/July 1961, and when Humphrey came home at the end of that year to attend the Imperial Defence College his success in running this 6000-strong station had added much to his growing reputation.

Another particularly challenging task followed three years later, after he had completed the IDC course and spent 1964 and 1965 in London in joint planning appointments. Already being marked as a potential CAS he was sent to Aden to succeed AVM "Johnnie" Johnson as AOC Air Forces Middle East and within two months of his arrival the British decision was announced to withdraw from Aden in 1968. The increase in terrorism, the loss of local support, the strain on the loyalty of the civil authorities, the need for continuous air operations of many kinds from the grossly overcrowded airfield at Khormaksar, the constant pressures of the security situation on all Service personnel: these and many more factors weighed heavily on him and his Army and Navy colleagues, yet when the actual withdrawal came in late 1967 (earlier than originally intended) it was accomplished with remarkable efficiency and success. His responsibilities had of course extended far beyond Aden itself, including air operations in the neighbouring protectorate, the maintenance of the RAF presence in the Gulf, support for the Beira patrol, and assistance to Zambia after the Rhodesian Declaration of Independence – all adding to his varied experience and helping prepare him for elevation to the Air Force Board.

His appointment as Air Member for Personnel in November 1967 was in some ways surprising, since his career so far had been very largely connected with operational flying and command, but he was delighted at last to have the chance to familiarise himself more closely with the many human aspects of his Service, and for three years he worked under John Grandy as CAS. Soon after his arrival the government announced its intention to withdraw from East of Suez, and much of his attention had to be devoted to preparing for the major cuts in manpower that would follow. The mergers of the UK Commands also had important personnel implications, but possibly more controversial was the decision to replace the traditional Cranwell cadet system by the Graduate Entry Scheme, under which all young GD officers awarded direct commissions would study for degrees at university before commencing flying training. The amalgamation of the Andover and Bracknell Staff Colleges in 1970 and the creation of the General Duties Aerosystems Course at Manby were other major changes, and on the inter-Service front there were the complex negotiations leading to the decision to introduce the military salary. Meanwhile his life-long enthusiasm for athletics had led to his becoming President of the RAF Athletics Association, and he remained until his death a constant supporter of all its activities.

At the end of 1970 he left the Air Force Board to take over Strike Command from Denis Spotswood, and he spent the next three years at High Wycombe, where the merger with Air Support Command in 1972 was soon to make him the first commander with responsibility for the entire operational air force in the United Kingdom. He soon familiarised himself with every role, visiting his many stations, flying the various aircraft whenever possible, and winning the confidence and respect of all his aircrew. He made time, too, for the many support staffs, fully appreciating that all were important. He also set great store by strengthening the ties with the other Services and with NATO; in particular he realised the need to work out joint operating procedures with the Royal Navy. At the same time he knew from his time as AMP how strong were the pressures for financial savings, and his Strike Command Economy Project was designed to make more resources available for the front line and demonstrate that the RAF was not wasting the taxpayers' money. But his most important task, as he saw it, was to reverse the run-down of the United Kingdom's air defences that had taken place in the 1960s, which entailed not just more fighter aircraft but also the up-dating of the command and control system and the long-term solution of the airborne early warning problem, and it was issues of this kind that continued to engage his attention when he became CAS in April 1974.

Andrew Humphrey served less time than most as CAS, but since his two years four months in office coincided with a major Defence Review instituted by the new Labour Government his was a particularly trying period. Underlying the Review was the desire for progressive savings in defence expenditure as a proportion of the Gross National Product, and the decisions to withdraw most of Britain's residual forces from overseas and to concentrate almost entirely on NATO commitments led to substantial cuts in the RAF front-line, most notably in the air transport force. The consequent closure of a number of home stations and major reductions in manpower – including a compulsory redundancy programme – were hard measures to take, and Humphrey felt keenly about their impact upon RAF morale. On the other hand many positive changes were taking place: the Jaguar was becoming operational and the Phantoms being switched to air defence, the Victor was being introduced in the tanker role, the programme to stretch the Hercules was underway, the Hawk was soon to enter service, and the MRCA prototypes were now flying. Further changes in the RAF organisation were also in progress, with Headquarters Near East Air Force being closed and its remaining forces passing to Strike Command, and Training and Support Commands shortly to be merged. But although there were grounds for some optimism about the future, Humphrey's chief concern remained the state of NATO's air defences and he spoke out openly about the implications of the defence cuts.

Sir Andrew was appointed Chief of the Defence Staff on 24 October 1976, having long been marked as the obvious successor. He died just three months later of pneumonia, soon after being taken ill following a visit to the armed forces in Norway in very cold weather. This was tragic not just for the RAF but for the Services as a whole and indeed the nation, and one can only speculate on what he, certainly one of the most professional aviators ever to reach the top of his Service, might still have achieved.

Marshal of the Royal Air Force
The Lord Cameron

Of all the distinguished officers who have held the post of CAS none had a more humble start than Lord Cameron, and his achievement becomes the more remarkable when one recalls that he went on to become Chief of the Defence Staff, to be raised to the Peerage, and to head one of the University of London's best known Colleges. Even more surprising, and hidden from most of his contemporaries, for much of his life he waged a battle with ill-health.

Neil Cameron was born in Perth in 1920 of a Scots Presbyterian family and on leaving school at 16 joined the Commercial Bank of Scotland – without enthusiasm – as an apprentice clerk. Much more interesting was the intensive flying activity at the RAF's Elementary Flying School at Scone and by joining the RAF Volunteer Reserve he was able to join in the fun. His serious training began in May 1939 and having learnt to fly the Tiger Moth he was called up on the outbreak of war and sent with his RAFVR colleagues to Hastings. After a frustrating six months of ground training he went to the EFTS at Redhill in March 1940 and thence to the SFTS at Montrose, where he almost wrote off his aircraft by illicit low-flying and forfeited his chances of a commission. The dire shortage of pilots in August 1940 ensured that no worse fate befell him, and after learning to fly the Hurricane at Aston Down he joined 1 Squadron at Wittering at the end of September, moving on to 17 Squadron at Martlesham Heath on 15 October. Two days later he was operational, in time for the closing fortnight of the Battle of Britain.

Sergeant Pilot Cameron spent nine months with 17 Squadron, first carrying out defensive operations over the coastal area and in support of North Sea convoys; then from Croydon patrolling over the south coast; and finally providing air defence from airfields in northern Scotland. Then, in July 1941, having at last secured his commission, he and some of his colleagues were sent to Leconfield to form the nucleus of the new 134 Squadron which was being despatched to Murmansk, in North Russia, as part of 151 Wing. The next four months were memorable among other things for two journeys with the Royal Navy, a carrier take-off without previous practice, air operations against the Luftwaffe in most difficult circumstances, and the experience of working with the Russians, to whom the Hurricanes were eventually handed over. Cameron would not have missed it for the world.

No 134 Squadron, re-equipped with Spitfires, was now ordered first to Northern Ireland and then in March 1942 to the Middle East. After a long sea journey via the Cape, Cameron eventually found himself in July back with a Hurricane squadron, 213, in the Western Desert, where he played his part in the battles of Alam Halfa and El Alamein, and in the follow-up operations during the Army's advance to Tripoli – not least when his squadron operated briefly from behind enemy lines. He would never forget this experience of the value of close land/air co-operation. His operational tour ended in March 1943, when he went for six months to train 335 Hellenic Squadron at Mersa Matruh.

Keen to return to more active operations, Cameron was now sent to India, where after a short spell in the fighter operations cell at Headquarters 224 Group, Chittagong, he was selected to command 258 Squadron, equipped with Hurricanes and based on the Arakan coast not far from the Japanese front. Its role was to strafe enemy positions, escort bomber and transport aircraft, and provide air defence, and he not only carried out his full share of operational sorties but also built up close relations with the Army. In mid-1944, with the Hurricanes now somewhat outdated, 258 Squadron was re-equipped with the Thunderbolt, and by November the necessary re-training was complete and the squadron back in action in the rapidly developing Burma campaign. It operated intensively for the next six months, up to the fall of Rangoon, carrying out every kind of ground attack operation, and with Cameron himself usually leading it. He left for home in August 1945, armed with the DFC and DSO, and the recipient of the warmest tributes from his squadron.

Neil Cameron had now been on operations nearly five years, most of them overseas, and was one of the RAF's most experienced fighter and ground attack pilots. Yet he was only just 25, was not a regular officer, and had no other qualifications. His first posting, however, was appropriately enough to the School of Air Support at Old Sarum, and when offered a permanent commission he immediately accepted. As he himself admitted, he found it difficult to settle down to the peacetime routines and rituals, but taking up rugby gave an outlet for his energies, and there was good advice to hand. So after 2½ years at Old Sarum and six months as RAF liaison officer at Headquarters Rhine Army in Germany he was selected to attend the course at the RAF Staff College, Andover; he had so far had hardly any staff experience and this was an eye-opener. Hardly surprisingly, a posting followed to the Air Ministry, in the Directorate of Organisation, in May 1949.

Six months later, after a rugby match, he was taken ill with sub-acute bacterial endocarditis, a disease of the heart valve, and spent much of the next two years in hospital, his life at times in the balance. Eventually, after what he always maintained was a miracle cure, he was able to resume his career in the General Duties Branch, though restricted in the type of flying he could undertake, so in 1951 he was posted to aircrew selection duties in London and then, in 1953, to the Directing Staff at Bracknell. Here he spent three very important years; building on his experience as a student at Andover he now had the opportunity to read deeply, to think about many of the issues of air power, to exchange ideas with others, and to write. His next posting was to command London University Air Squadron; in providing the entrée into the academic environment this enabled him to continue his intellectual develop-ment, while at the same time allowing him to fly again. His squadron won the Hack Trophy in 1957, an achievement which gave him particular satisfaction.

That his potential was now becoming recognised was shown in late 1958 when he was chosen to become Personal Staff Officer to the CAS, and for the next two years working first under Dermot Boyle and then Tom Pike he had an ideal opportunity to learn the workings of the Air Ministry, to get to know many of the leading personalities, and to become conversant with the great issues of the day during a period when the RAF was striving to recover from the effects of the Sandys Defence Review. He also found time to win the Gordon Shephard Prize Essay competition, the subject being the need for a deterrent force, before he moved on in October 1960 to take command of RAF Abingdon. This was the home of the RAF's two home-based Beverley squadrons, 47 and 53, and his two years there saw constant operational activity, much of it routine but also including flood relief operations in East Africa and – most notably – the reinforcement of Kuwait in July 1961. Cameron's interest in his transport squadrons was matched by his enthusiasm for the work of 1 Parachute Training School, and he was delighted that so many of his responsibilities entailed co-operation with the Army, reminding him of his wartime days. He ended what had been a particularly happy tour in December 1962, following it with a year at the Imperial Defence College, and another year working again as PSO to Tom Pike, now in Paris as Deputy SACEUR.

On returning home he was chosen to go to Cranwell as Assistant Commandant (Cadets) in May 1965; while further major changes in the Cranwell system were now being mooted, his main task during his relatively short stay was to help oversee the merger of the Cranwell and Henlow Colleges, with their respective cadet schemes. A very different but equally demanding challenge faced him in September 1966, when he was summoned to the MOD to join Denis Healey's Programme Evaluation Group as the RAF member; his growing reputation as an independent-minded thinker had clearly had some impact. He spent four years working for Healey, first directly in PEG and then, when PEG was realised to be causing difficulties to the Chiefs of Staff, indirectly as head of the new Joint Planning Staff. Cameron, a firm believer in the importance of taking an overall defence view on the many strategic issues of the day, some of which were dividing the three Services, found this a particularly stimulating period, and he and Healey had much respect for each other.

He was, however, viewed with considerable suspicion by some of his RAF contemporaries, who felt he was insufficiently supportive of the light-blue arguments over such issues as the need for the F-111, and when he left the Ministry of Defence in 1970 for what he considered "a peripheral appointment" as SASO at Headquarters Air Support Command, it seemed to him that he was being penalised for this and was unlikely to advance much further. Nevertheless Upavon was hardly a backwater; it was responsible not just for the air transport force but also for the RAF's ground attack Phantoms and Harriers, roles entirely appropriate to Cameron's earlier experience. Nor was his next appointment, Deputy Commander in RAF Germany, quite as marginal as he seems to have thought, for it gave him responsibility for the day-to-day running of the RAF's major overseas command. He stayed there only a year before returning home in December 1973 as AOC 46 Group, delighted that – notwithstanding some further medical problems – his career was again taking off, and attributing this largely to the influence of his new CinC, Andrew Humphrey. A mere ten months later Humphrey, now CAS, brought him to the MOD as his Air Member for Personnel.

He arrived at a time when a defence review instituted by the new Labour Government was about to lead to major cuts in the RAF front line, particularly in the air transport force, and his primary task was to organise the consequent 18% reduction in manpower. Realising there were no painless solutions and accepting that some compulsory redundancy was inevitable, he insisted on the programme going quickly ahead, while doing his utmost to explain it and ensure that the individuals involved were properly treated. Although he was heavily involved in many other personnel matters, often jointly with his Navy and Army colleagues on such things as pay, his spell as AMP was dominated by the redundancy issue and he always regretted its necessity.

Neil Cameron succeeded Andrew Humphrey in August 1976; admittedly he had a restricted medical category and had never been a Commander-in-Chief, but his wartime record, his reputation for independent and constructive thinking, and his very wide range of experience, especially in the ways of Whitehall, made him the obvious choice. Assuming that he had three or more years ahead of him, he saw one of his tasks as improving communication and rebuilding confidence within the RAF; another was to encourage the spread of air power thinking, and to warn the nation at large of the seriousness and scale of the growing Soviet air threat. By his own trenchant lecturing, by the institution of a regular Commanders' Brief, by the establishment of a Director of Defence Studies, for example, he made a good start, but the work on which he had set his heart was cut short when, following the untimely death of Andrew Humphrey, it became clear that he would shortly be moved upwards to become Chief of the Defence Staff. So after just a year, in which he had busied himself not just with purely RAF affairs but also alongside the other Chiefs of Staff on such matters as the pay review and the reinforcement of the garrison in Belize, he carried out his last function as CAS, the Silver Jubilee Review of the RAF at Finningley on 29 July 1977. It was a proud moment.

Neil Cameron became CDS in September, taking over from Admiral of the Fleet Sir Edward Ashmore, who had held the post since Andrew Humphrey's death. It was, of course, the last appointment he could ever have expected, and though he filled it for only two years he established a reputation as a particularly courageous and forthright Chief, not afraid to engage in public controversy. When the Services came to the rescue during the firemen's strike in late 1977 he led the other Chiefs to see the Prime Minister to urge the case for the Armed Forces also to be given pay comparability, and the eventual achievement of this in 1979 owed much to his determination and ability to "work the system" with his uniformed and civilian colleagues. He continued to take every opportunity to lecture on defence subjects, surveying the inter-national scene with considerable perception and stressing the alarming growth of Soviet military power and his belief in nuclear deterrence – which he could always reconcile with his strongly held Christian beliefs. He travelled too, visiting Iran shortly before the overthrow of the Shah and – more significantly – China. The first NATO Defence Chief to tour the People's Republic, he roused the ire of the Russians, and the protests of the Labour left-wing, by his reference to "the common enemy at the door", but attempts to force his dismissal were firmly rejected by Mr Callaghan's government.

He retired as CDS in August 1979 and a year later fulfilled a life-long ambition by joining the world of academe, as Principal of King's College London. Having quickly earned the respect and affection of his new colleagues he was soon immersed in the major issues arising from the restructuring of London University, and the successful merger of King's with Queen Elizabeth and Chelsea Colleges in 1985 owed much to his drive and wisdom. Yet he still found time for many other interests: in the Service sphere he continued his support for the RAF Rugby Union, presided over the RAF Club, and chaired the Trustees of the RAF Museum; elsewhere he presided over the British Atlantic Committee, chaired the Trident Trust, and played leading roles in a number of Christian organizations; and he started work on his autobiography.

In 1983 his many achievements were recognized by the award of a Life Peerage, and a year later Lord Cameron of Balhousie was further honoured when he became a Knight of the Thistle. Sadly, however, he was now losing his long fight against ill-health, and having survived two major operations in 1982 and 1984 he died of cancer in January 1985. Not just the RAF but a much wider community had lost a fine leader and a good friend.

Marshal of the Royal Air Force
Sir Michael Beetham

Rarely in recent times has a Chief had the opportunity to preside over the RAF during a significant military conflict, though all have had to be ready for one. For Sir Michael Beetham, however, the possibility became a reality in April 1982 when Argentina invaded the Falkland Islands, and as the last CAS to have flown in face of the enemy in the Second World War he could well appreciate the possible consequences of the decisions that had to be made.

Michael Beetham was born in London in May 1923 and educated at St Marylebone Grammar School. Then in 1941, having witnessed some of the action during the Battle of Britain, he saw the RAF as the obvious place for him and was accepted for pilot training. The earlier part he did under the Arnold Scheme in the United States in 1942, following up with operational training as a bomber pilot in England during 1943, first on Wellingtons and then on Lancasters. By November he was ready to join 50 Squadron at Skellingthorpe, just in time for one of the most hard-fought phases of the bomber offensive, the Battle of Berlin. He flew his Lancaster to Berlin itself no less than ten times, lost an engine over Augsburg, and took part in the ill-fated Nuremberg Raid, but it was on a daylight training flight in February 1944 that he came nearest to disaster, when an engine caught fire and he and his crew had to bale out near East Kirkby. He promptly joined the Caterpillar Club.

His first operational tour safely completed, he was switched to flying instructional duties in May 1944, and although later selected to join 57 Squadron, based coincidentally at East Kirkby, the European war was almost over. He was, however, just in time to help in dropping supplies to the Dutch and bringing home the prisoners-of-war, whereupon his squadron, about to convert to the Lincoln, was earmarked for Tiger Force in order to operate from Okinawa against Japan. The ending of the Far Eastern war soon put paid to that scheme, and in November 1945 Beetham returned to the Lancaster when he joined 35 Squadron, based at Graveley, as a Flight Commander. This was a fortunate move, since his new squadron was shortly chosen to take part in the Victory Fly-Past and the RAF's goodwill tour of the USA, and he and his colleagues brought their display flying to a very high standard.

Having now been selected for a permanent commission, he was moved to a personnel staff appointment at Headquarters Bomber Command in 1947, and – apart from a tour of the USA with the CinC, as his acting ADC – spent most of his time looking after aircrew postings. It was invaluable experience, gained at a particularly difficult time for the Command in the aftermath of the war, and he felt he had earned his subsequent move to 82 Squadron in August 1949. Here he worked for two years as a detachment commander, flying Lancasters on the aerial mapping survey of British Africa, working for much of the time alongside another future CAS, Andrew Humphrey*, and extending not only his flying skills but also his knowledge of the problems of command. On returning home he was destined for the Canberra force, but thanks to its delayed arrival found himself attending the Andover Staff Course in 1952 and – almost inevitably – moving to the Air Ministry in 1953.

For the next three years he worked in the Operational Requirements Branch, involved with all the RAF's bomber and reconnaissance aircraft. The problems of bringing the V-bombers into service took much of his time: for example could both the Vulcan and the Victor be accepted; could one have a bomber without defensive armament; could one agree to there being no means of assisted escape for the rear crew? There were longer term matters also, notably the TSR 2 for which Beetham drafted the first specification and which in his view should never have been abandoned. Most significant of all for his future career were the atomic weapons trials at Maralinga, known as Operation Buffalo, which he attended in 1956 as Personal Staff Officer to the Task Force Commander; the witnessing of these four mighty explosions had a major influence on all his later strategic thinking, convincing him that it would never be practicable to impose limits on a nuclear war.

On returning from Australia he was selected to join the V-bomber force that was now entering service, and after a year of conversion training he took over command of 214 Squadron at Marham from Wing Commander Trent, the wartime VC. Equipped with the Valiant, part of the squadron was about to convert to the air-to-air refuelling role, and in 1959, after a full year of trials and training, they were ready to make a name for themselves with a number of special long-distance flights. These culminated in July, when Beetham himself piloted a Valiant the 6060 miles to Cape Town in under 11½ hours and returned a few days later in under 12½ hours. These, the first non-stop flights between England and Cape Town, broke the speed record for the distance and provided a convincing demonstration of the feasibility and potential of AAR. Yet it was not – as originally intended – to extend the range of the V-bombers that AAR was now to be developed in the RAF, but to increase the endurance of the fighters. It would take the Falklands War to mark the fulfilment of the concept.

Now almost totally a Bomber Command man, he was to spend four years at the centre of its affairs, firstly at 3 Group as Wing Commander Operations and then at the Headquarters, mostly as Group Captain Operations, working under Sir Kenneth Cross and later Sir John Grandy. These were challenging years, with the V-force at the heart of the nation's defences and receiving the highest priority for resources, and very high professional standards were set and achieved. The most critical moment came with the Cuban Missile Crisis in October 1962, when the Thor missiles and V-bombers were held at the highest permissible degree of readiness amid an outside world which, as Beetham remembers, seemed to have little idea of what was at stake. Yet during these years there were new concepts to face. The shooting down of Gary Powers' U2 aircraft over the Soviet Union spelt the end of the 'fast and high' doctrine; to penetrate in future Bomber Command would have to go in low, entailing loss of range and the need for pop-up delivery; then came Nassau, the unwelcome

* See page 76

cancellation of Skybolt, and the decision to switch eventually to Polaris. Here were massive implications for Bomber Command and indeed the RAF, and Beetham was deeply involved in the staff work.

In 1964 came a complete change of scene, when at the request of AVM 'Johnnie' Johnson, the AOC, he was sent to command Khormaksar, then the RAF's biggest overseas station and operating almost every type of aircraft except Beetham's own speciality, the bomber. His arrival in November virtually coincided with the start of a major terrorist campaign against the British forces in Aden, and throughout his two years there the security of his overcrowded station was his biggest preoccupation; he was insistent that everyone must share the inevitable guard duties. At the same time Khormaksar was an important staging post on the route to the Far East, and many of the hundred or so aircraft based there were engaged in operations in the neighbouring Radfan; he himself took every opportunity to fly with the squadrons, and gained more varied experience than at any time in his career.

A year at the Imperial Defence College followed, which among other things gave him the chance to see something of Eastern Europe, and in 1968 he returned to Whitehall to work again in Operational Requirements, where he was responsible for some 126 equipment programmes and this time had to exist alongside the new staff superstructures of the central Ministry of Defence. Eleven months later, having just found his way around and established all the necessary contacts in industry, he was somewhat frustratingly switched to become Director of Strike Operations, where he spent the next two years handling day-to-day events. This was a relatively quiet period for the RAF, marked mainly by the progressive withdrawal from East of Suez and by Colonel Gadaffi's arrival on the scene in Libya, but there was still plenty to do, and the post provided good preparation for his next tour as Commandant of the RAF Staff College. The separate Colleges at Andover and Bracknell had just been combined, with the incorporation of overseas students in the main course presenting a new challenge, but at the same time there were insistent pressures for economies and while he was determined to preserve the wider purposes of staff college training he had reluctantly to accept a reduction in the length of the course.

Beetham left Bracknell in August 1972 to become Assistant Chief of Staff (Plans and Policy) at SHAPE, in Belgium. The first British officer to fill this particularly important post – negotiated by the CAS, Denis Spotswood* – he stayed there nearly three years, working first under General Goodpaster and then General Haig, and took part in all the NATO planning. This was a period when much work was being done to build up NATO's conventional forces in accordance with the strategy of flexible response and much was achieved, not least in the hardening programme and the improvement of communications. There was much work involved, including many visits, and Beetham gained invaluable experience of working with officers of the many other nations in the Alliance. He returned home in 1975 for what turned out to be a brief spell as Deputy Commander-in-Chief at Strike Command, which gave him an ideal opportunity to up-date himself on the RAF's front-line and in particular to familiarise himself with the aircraft he would be responsible for as CinC RAF

* See page 74

Germany and Commander 2 ATAF, where he was to go in January 1976.

Already conversant with much of the German scene from his years at SHAPE, he was now in charge of one of NATO's main air forces and one of his chief concerns was to co-ordinate its operations with those at 4 ATAF to the south. Close links with BAOR, too, were essential, and although there were differences over such matters as support helicopters, he and General King got on extremely well together; the forward deployment of the Harriers to Gutersloh, made possible when the Lightnings were replaced by air defence Phantoms, was much to the Army's liking. Because of Beetham's many NATO responsibilities the RAF in Germany was run day-to-day mainly by his Deputy Commander; the hardening programme was now almost complete, the Taceval system was working well though making great demands, and there were the inevitable difficulties over low flying, which necessitated regular contact with the local community. Berlin, seen under different circumstances thirty years earlier, also required regular visits, and there were periodic polite but superficial meetings with his Soviet opposite number. He had, however, been in Germany little more than a year when he heard the sad news of Andrew Humphrey's death, and before long he knew that Neil Cameron's selection as CDS had put him in line to succeed him as CAS. Almost certainly the post would have been his anyway a year or two later, but through taking over in August 1977 he was set for a term of office longer than those of any of his predecessors barring Trenchard.

Recognising that the heavy cuts his predecessors had been compelled to impose had seriously impaired morale, he saw among his main initial tasks the restoration of some stability and the further improvement of communication within the RAF; his many visits to stations, his institution of regular station commanders' conferences, and the formation of the RAF Presentation Team all contributed to this end, and to the wider dissemination of the air power message. More specifically he also had to address himself, along with his Chiefs of Staff colleagues, to the problems of Service pay, which were now seriously hindering recruitment and causing an exodus of skilled people. Fortunately, thanks to the publicity gained during the firemen's strike a substantial pay award and a new pay deal were achieved in 1978, thus removing one of his greatest anxieties. Another serious challenge, however, lay ahead, for fairly soon after the election of the Thatcher government in 1979 it was decided to carry out a major defence review. Unlike previous reviews, which had always had the option of cutting overseas commitments, that now to be conducted by John Nott had no choice but to concentrate on Britain's contribution to NATO, and the eventual decision to economise mainly in the Navy's surface fleet largely accorded with Beetham's own views, since he believed the maritime threat could best be countered predominantly by a mix of under-water and airborne weapons.

While these and other major issues such as the purchase of Trident and the deployment of cruise missiles were being debated at Chiefs of Staff level, there were many RAF matters also engaging his attention. The strike version of the Tornado had just entered service, and he had to defend it against much unjustified criticism in its early stages. Air defence was still far from satisfactory, and it was decided to run on the Lightning and arm the Hawk. The purchase of the Chinook and the stretching of the Hercules were other important measures, and although the decision to order the AEW Nimrod had been taken before his time it was one which he continued to support. He was also keen on trying to build up the RAF's reserve strength, and a start was made with the Regiment squadrons of the Royal Auxiliary Air Force. On the other hand, much as he wanted to revive the Cranwell cadet scheme, he was unable to do so.

By 1982 his hand-over was approaching, and only one relatively minor military operation had marked his tour of office – Agila, the Rhodesian monitoring operation of 1979/1980. Then, almost out of the blue, came the Argentine invasion of the Falkland Islands, and as Acting Chief of the Defence Staff, (CDS, Sir Terence Lewin, was abroad at the time) Beetham was immediately involved in the decision to send the Task Force. Needless to say he fully supported it, while pointing out the threat it would face from land-based air power, and in Chiefs of Staff discussions throughout the campaign he urged that the major ships should as far as possible be kept out of range of air attack. Insistent that the RAF should contribute as much as possible to the operation, he ensured that it was properly represented at the various levels of command, and took close interest in its many activities – not least the Vulcan operations against Stanley Airfield, only made possible by the in-flight refuelling techniques which he himself had done so much to pioneer many years before.

Sir Michael Beetham handed over as CAS a few months afterwards, in October 1982, and has since divided his time between GEC Avionics of which he was until recently Chairman, and various RAF connections, notably the RAF Museum where he has been a particularly active Chairman of the Trustees since 1983.

Marshal of the Royal Air Force
Sir Keith Williamson

If one of Trenchard's greatest legacies was the RAF College at Cranwell, from which he hoped many of its Chiefs would eventually come, another was the Aircraft Apprentice Scheme, designed to prepare the technical tradesmen on whose skill the Service would for ever depend. There has always been a channel for the most promising of these apprentices to move on to the RAF College and thus enter the permanent cadre of the General Duties Branch, but although over the years some of these have reached very senior rank only one has made it to the top: Sir Keith Williamson.

He was born at Leytonstone in February 1928, and remembers as a twelve-year old watching the dog-fights that went on over Essex during the Battle of Britain. When his school in Woodford was bombed, however, he was evacuated to Leicestershire, where until 1944 he attended Market Harborough Grammar School and joined 1084 Squadron of the Air Training Corps. Then, just before his 17th birthday, he enlisted at Halton as an Aircraft Apprentice and being keen to study radio spent the next three years at the Radio School, at that time located at Cranwell. On qualifying as an Air Radio Fitter in 1948 he was immediately offered a Flight Cadetship at the RAF College, and he graduated as a pilot at the end of 1950. Not surprisingly these six years at Cranwell gave him a lasting affection for it, and he greatly regrets that the RAF chose to depart from the traditional Flight Cadet system.

From Cranwell, delighted to have been selected to become a fighter pilot, he went straight to the Advanced Flying School at Driffield, where he learnt to fly first the Meteor and then the Vampire, and had the risks of flying jet aircraft in those early days brought home to him by the high accident rate. He himself survived unscathed and in July 1951 went to Germany to join 112 Squadron, based first at Fassberg and then Jever. In some ways this first flying tour was the best time of his life, for the Vampire was marvellous to fly, the squadron had to maintain a high degree of readiness in face of the Soviet threat, and he was serving under such charismatic commanders as Teddy Donaldson and Johnnie Johnson. He returned home after 18 months to attend a Pilot Attack Instructors course and then, along with many of his contemporaries, volunteered for service in Korea.

Apart from its three Sunderland Squadrons, the RAF had little opportunity to contribute directly to the Korean war, but a number of its pilots were allowed to serve with the United States and Australian squadrons and Williamson was chosen to join 77 Squadron of the RAAF, equipped with Meteors. Since the Meteor had been totally outclassed by the MIG 15, by the time he arrived it had been switched to the ground attack role, for which it was not well suited. By now the war was almost over and he was able to fly only a handful of operational sorties before the cease-fire in July 1953. He remained in Korea several more months before returning home to White Waltham to become ADC to the AOCinC Home Command, Sir Harold Lydford, an appointment that he viewed with some dismay. Nevertheless, he now accepts that he learnt much from the experience.

He left Home Command in April 1956, and after completing a Hunter conversion course returned to 112 Squadron, now based at Bruggen. His hopes of a rewarding second flying tour were, however, quickly dashed when the Sandys White Paper of 1957 led, among other things, to the RAF in Germany losing 16 of its 33 squadrons, including the whole Bruggen Wing. Fortunately he was quickly chosen to become a Flight Commander on another Hunter squadron, 20, based at Oldenburg; otherwise he might well have left the RAF at that point, as did many of his contemporaries. This was indeed the low point of his career. In face of an undiminished Soviet threat the nation's air defences had been almost irretrievably damaged, as he saw it, for essentially political reasons.

Returning home from Germany in 1958 he volunteered for the Central Flying School and having qualified as a flying instructor spent over three years first in command of 1 Squadron at 2 Flying Training School, Syerston, and then at CFS Little Rissington as an examiner. By 1962 he was ready for the mind-broadening opportunities offered by the Staff College and having thoroughly enjoyed his year at Bracknell was given his first posting to the Air Ministry, shortly to become part of the Ministry of Defence. He stayed there until mid-1965, working in the Air Secretary's Department, where he was responsible initially for the affairs of some of the more junior pilots and then for the appointments and careers of all Wing Commanders of the General Duties Branch. Working very long hours, he found it a rewarding job, providing excellent insight into the way the RAF managed its own most precious resource, its people.

By now he was due for a return to operational flying and after a series of courses, the main one at Coltishall learning to fly the Lightning, he took command of 23 Squadron, based at Leuchars. He recalls his two years there as one of the high-spots of his career; Leuchars was a particularly happy station led by a very good station commander in Group Captain John Nichols, and the Lightning was a potent fighting aircraft that was both exacting and delightful to fly. These were, of course, the final days of Fighter Command, now but a shadow of its former self, and as very much a fighter man Williamson viewed its merger into Strike Command in 1968 with very mixed feelings. He himself was destined to go elsewhere, his familiarity with the Lightning making him an obvious choice to take command of the RAF's most forward main base in Germany – Gutersloh. With NATO's strategy now changing to that of flexible response and the Soviet intervention in Czechoslovakia serving as a reminder of the Soviet threat, these were challenging years for RAF Germany, and not least for Gutersloh's two Lightning and two Hunter squadrons. To provide better airfield defence the base was now allocated an RAF Regiment squadron, and the Tactical Evaluation system – nowadays an integral part of RAF life – made its first appearance.

What would prove to be his final tour in Germany now complete, he spent 1971 attending the Royal College of Defence Studies, at that time under a civilian Commandant, Alistair Buchan, before returning to the Ministry of

Defence to carry out a study into the vulnerability of the Linesman air defence system. Then in September 1972 he was appointed Director of Air Plans, which exposed him for the first time to the pressures of working in the Main Building and to the often partisan attitudes of the three Services. With extensive restructuring in progress following the main withdrawals from East of Suez, and with a major defence review under way, there was much to do if the RAF's core programme was to be protected. At the heart of the RAF's major re-equipment plans lay the Tornado and the RAF was successful in defending this; in other respects, however, Williamson felt the Service made too many unilateral and painful economies which did nothing to protect it from later cuts imposed on all three Services.

Now all too well aware of the importance of astute staff work, he was a good choice to become Commandant of the Staff College in 1975. Persuaded of its mind-broadening function from his own time there as a student, he was convinced that the reduced six-month course was too short, and by the time he departed in 1977 he had made the case for the phased reintroduction of the longer course that survives to this day. His next move, which took place at short notice, was to give him his first direct experience of the international scene, for he went to SHAPE as Assistant Chief of Staff in the Plans and Policy Division. Having to work with the Americans and with officers from many European nations was an education in itself, and with the NATO Defence Ministers agreeing that expenditure must be increased in face of the improving capability of the Soviet forces there was much staff activity – though Williamson often wondered about its effectiveness.

He came home in August 1978 and – unusually for a future CAS – took over as Commander-in-Chief RAF Support Command. Apart from flying and staff training this was a totally new world to him, affording him the ideal opportunity to familiarise himself with the multifarious activities on which a modern Air Force depends. The major problems then being faced in recruiting and retaining the right kind of personnel were putting the training machine under much pressure, and the consequent reopening of the flying training school at Church Fenton was a sizeable task. At the same time the Gnat and Hunter were being replaced by the Hawk. Two further changes during his time at Brampton were the introduction of a highly successful scheme to give junior airmen proper training for NCO rank, and the extension to RAF Support Command of the Tactical Evaluation system; he had mixed feelings about this, for while recognising the need for his units to be militarily prepared he was worried lest his Command's ability to meet its demanding training and production targets might be jeopardised.

After two very happy years he moved on again, this time to take over Strike Command at High Wycombe. Initially somewhat apprehensive about the sheer size of the structure, he soon found that it was soundly organised, and since he could draw on the specialist expertise at each of the Group Headquarters he felt it was not difficult to control. Many improvements were under way, with the Tornado and Chinook being introduced, the Phantom being upgraded and the Hawk being armed, and he himself had to spend considerable time on helping along the new ground environment for the home air defence system, known as UKADGE. Recollecting all too well how air defence had suffered at the hands of Duncan Sandys, he knew how difficult it

68 Pilot Officer Cameron (extreme right) with other pilots in Russia, late 1941.

69 Flight Lieutenant Cameron (back row, second from right) in the Andover Rugby XV, 1948/9.

70 *Sir Neil Cameron greets the Queen at the Silver Jubilee Review of the Royal Air Force at Finningley, July 1977.*

71 *Sir Neil Cameron, as Chief of the Defence Staff, on his visit to China.*

72 Sir Michael Beetham flies the Harrier, 1978.   *73 Sir Michael Beetham visits Gutersloh, 1980.*

74 Sir Michael Beetham visits Ascension Island in June 1982, at the end of the Falklands Conflict.

75 *Flight Lieutenant Williamson climbing into the cockpit of a Meteor of 77 Squadron, RAAF, in Korea, 1953.*

76 *Air Vice-Marshal Williamson at SHAPE bidding farewell to SACEUR, General Haig, July 1978.*

77 *Sir Keith Williamson with General Rogers, SACEUR, at Headquarters Strike Command, October 1980.*

78 Sir Keith Williamson welcomes the Prime Minister and Mr Thatcher to Cranwell for the Queen's Review, July 1983.

79 Air Vice-Marshal Craig visits Waddington to present the Most-improved Piper Cup to Neil McDougall, May 1979.

80 *Sir David Craig visits RAF Stanley in 1983. With him (left to right) are Group Captain Austin, General Thorne and Group Captain Wilson.*

81 *Sir David Craig accompanies the Queen Mother from a ceremony at the Law Courts. Air Chief Marshal Sir Christopher Foxley-Norris is on the Queen Mother's right.*

82 *Air Vice-Marshal Craig conducts a WRAF passing-out parade at RAF Henlow.*

83 *Sir David Craig with General Von Senger, CINCENT, 1983.*

84 *MRAF Sir David Craig, Chief of the Defence Staff, with his Chiefs of Staff colleagues, 1990. Left to right: General Sir Richard Vincent (VCDS), General Sir John Chappell (CGS), Sir David Craig, Admiral Sir Julian Oswald (First Sea Lord), Air Chief Marshal Sir Peter Harding (CAS).*

had been to reawaken the politicians and indeed the other Services to the extent of the Soviet air threat, but by now at least some of the RAF's planning in the later 1960s and 1970s was coming to fruition and he was delighted to be able to help resuscitate the system. He was hardly enamoured, however, of the procurement organisation, which seemed to lack clear lines of responsibility and only to compound the difficulties and delays inevitable in such large and complex projects.

Part of his time had to be spent fulfilling his NATO duties as Commander-in-Chief UK Air, meeting with and getting to know the other Major Subordinate Commanders; he also had to maintain Strike Command's important ties with the United States Air Force; and there were regular contacts with his opposite numbers in the Royal Navy and Army. To his concern, however, the other Services all too often appeared to have insufficient understanding of the importance of air power, and this view was reinforced by much of what he saw during the Falklands campaign of 1982, when he wished there had been a senior air adviser at sea with the Task Force to mastermind the day-to-day air activities. Nevertheless aircraft from his Command, including Vulcans, Victors, Harriers, Nimrods, Hercules, VC 10s and helicopters, all played important roles, and he was disappointed that their contributions were not better understood by the wider public. While most of the RAF's support for the Task Force was directed by one of his Group Commanders, Sir John Curtiss, at Northwood, he and his staff at High Wycombe were heavily committed throughout, providing the necessary back-up and often assisting with the planning.

A few months later, he succeeded Sir Michael Beetham as Chief of the Air Staff. While he had not served on the Air Force Board, he was in all other respects well qualified for the appointment, though he had never really expected it to come his way. The defence scene in October 1982, when he took over, was still largely dominated by the aftermath of the Falklands War, and he took an early opportunity to visit the islands in order to judge the local situation for himself. Quickly realising that an effective air defence was critical if they were to be protected against a further Argentine air attack, he insisted that a force of eight Phantoms must be based there and that modern ground radars must be installed. At the same time he recognised that the present runway at Stanley, even if extended as was then being proposed, could never be raised to full operational standards; it took another year, however, to persuade the government that the only real solution was to build an entirely new airfield at Mount Pleasant. These and many other residual matters from the Falklands conflict were important preoccupations throughout Williamson's three years in office.

Most of the RAF's other activities during this time were relatively routine, but the famine-relief operations in Ethiopia, Operation Bushel, brought the RAF very good publicity, as did the brief demonstration by a flight of Buccaneers over Beirut in 1983.

Inevitably much of his time was spent on longer-term issues. The Jet Provost, for example, was due for replacement as the RAF's initial trainer, and with several aircraft in contention there was much debate before the decision was made to buy the Tucano. The negotiations to sell the Tornado to Saudi Arabia depended heavily on RAF support, and since Williamson was keen to capitalise on the aircraft's spectacular success in the Strategic Air Command bombing competition he backed it wholeheartedly. Another major project was the continuing development of the Airborne Early-Warning Nimrod; already there were many doubts about its viability but with the government still committed to it work had to proceed, and the Trials Unit was set up at Waddington. The most important project, however, was the European Fighter Aircraft, about which there was much negotiating both in the Ministry of Defence and between the participating nations, and Williamson was pleased to have been so closely involved in securing the necessary agreement.

One further major question arose during his time: the proposal by the Defence Secretary, Michael Heseltine, to further reorganise the Ministry of Defence. In essence this entailed the movement of the hitherto single-Service policy and operational requirements staffs into a much strengthened Central Staff under the Chief of the Defence Staff; it would leave each individual Chief of Staff responsible for little more than the efficient management of his own Service. Williamson, one of many who believed that centralisation had already gone far enough, was not persuaded that this restructuring was wise and made his views clearly known, as was his right. This was not the first time he had had experience of political decisions about military policy for reasons that, he felt, took too little account of the real needs of national defence. He still believes the reorganisation was ill-conceived; while it may appear to work satisfactorily in peacetime he fears it might be a different story in war.

Sir Keith relinquished the post in October 1985 and now devotes much time to the Presidency of the Royal Air Forces Association. He is also President of the Officers' Association, and Vice President of SSAFA. He lives in Norfolk, where golf and sailing are among his interests.

Marshal of the Royal Air Force
Sir David Craig

We come now to the last CAS in our series, Sir David Craig, appointed in 1985. Whereas all his 18 predecessors had flown in combat or held command in war, and many had done both, he had never been called on to act in anger. If at first this seems surprising, one must remember that since 1945 the United Kingdom has not often been involved in major wars, and from now on Sir David's career pattern is much more likely to prove the norm rather than the exception.

Like Sir Dermot Boyle he came from Southern Ireland, being born in Dublin in 1929, and much of the war largely passed him by, his main recollections being of an unrationed, unblacked out, neutral life. In 1943, however, he was sent to Radley, where he rowed, captained the First XV, became Head of School and finally qualified to read Mathematics at Oxford. His intention at that stage was to become a teacher and he was actually offered a post at Eton, but having joined the University Air Squadron – essentially for fun and to boost his income – he was acquiring a growing interest in aviation. The influence of his CO, Wing Commander Foxley-Norris, and also advice received from Sholto Douglas had their effect, and on graduating in 1951 he immediately joined the RAF with a permanent commission.

Direct entrants with his sort of qualifications were scarce in those days, and no time was wasted in putting him through the pilots' course at 7 Flying Training School at Cottesmore; he was awarded his "Wings" seven months later, in April 1952. He moved straight on to the Advanced Flying School at Driffield and then, instead of joining a squadron as he had expected, was chosen to become a flying instructor. Consequently in January 1953 he found himself at 209 Advanced Flying School at Weston Zoyland, where he remained for over two years; while some of his pupils were National Service trainees, others were piston-engined pilots of long experience who were undertaking jet conversion, and he relished the challenge – though as he reflects there were many accidents.

It was therefore 1955 before he reached his first front-line unit. 247 Squadron, which had distinguished itself with its Typhoons during the Normandy campaign, was at Odiham re-equipping from the Meteor to the Hunter when he joined it, and having completed the Day Fighter Leaders' course at West Raynham he came to appreciate much about tactics. There was plenty of exciting flying over the next couple of years, even though the aircraft were afflicted by engine surge problems, and for Craig it was a thoroughly enjoyable tour. In 1957, however, the scene changed. 247 was now destined for disbandment, the fate of so many of the RAF's fighter squadrons as a result of the Sandys Defence Review, and Craig's Mathematics degree made him an obvious candidate to enter the guided missile field in which the future of air defence was thought by some to lie. So after completing the Guided Weapons Course at the RAF Technical College, Henlow, and then at Manby, he found himself in October 1957 at

North Coates, the first test and evaluation unit for the Bloodhound, the RAF's new surface-to-air guided weapon. Unfortunately, however, little of the hardware had actually arrived, and he spent a frustrating 18 months there, unable to achieve anything really worthwhile; he never even saw a Bloodhound.

It was therefore with some relief that he heard in 1959 of his posting to the Air Ministry, even though his new task was to be in the same sphere, mainly planning the deployment of Bloodhound Mark II. This entailed much surveying of old airfields and subsequent drafting of staff papers and provided him with considerable insight into the ways of the Air Ministry, though he still had very little knowledge of what lay beyond the world of air defence. It was the Staff Course at Andover that followed in 1961 which first gave him the opportunity to think about the RAF as a whole and he found it a very worthwhile year. Half his course were high calibre officers from overseas and he made numerous friends who later held senior rank in their own Services.

A complete change now lay ahead. Like a number of other pilots whose careers had hitherto lain largely in air defence, he was chosen to switch to the V-bomber force, and after a series of conversion courses lasting for most of 1962 he joined 35 Squadron at Coningsby as a Flight Commander in January 1963. This squadron had had a proud wartime record in Bomber Command and until recently had been equipped with the Canberra; it was now being re-formed to operate the Vulcan II. Some three weeks after arriving, Craig and his crew were being checked by the squadron commander, who in very poor visibility decided to take over and try to land. On losing visual reference he struck the ground, damaging the undercarriage, and subsequently crash-landed at Waddington. For Craig this was the nearest he ever came to disaster in an aircraft, and in the aftermath he was appointed to take command of the squadron. So for the next two years he directed its build-up, first at Coningsby and then at Cottesmore, and played the leading role in all its activities; while it took its share of Quick Reaction Alert duties, it was also committed in the conventional role to Far East reinforcement, and with the Indonesian Confrontation at its height Craig and his crews spent some of their time in Singapore. The V-force was in his view demonstrating the "reach" that is one of the essential elements of air power and would be shown again in the Falklands campaign, this time with the aid of air-to-air refuelling. While 35 Squadron had that capability in the 1960s – he himself lost his probe on one occasion – it ceased AAR from then on. He handed over in June 1965 after an extremely busy and demanding tour, firmly convinced of the vital role being played by the V-force in the nation's defence.

It was now time for a further broadening of his horizons, and his appointment as Military Assistant to the Chief of the Defence Staff provided an excellent opportunity. Working first for Field Marshal Sir Richard Hull and then for a few months for Sir Charles Elworthy, he saw at first hand many of the policy changes of the Healey period and recalls particularly the drama of the carrier controversy. By the time he departed in early 1968 he had acquired invaluable knowledge of the Ministry of Defence, its methods and its personalities, and had also travelled to many parts of the world, gaining in the process an extensive military and diplomatic education. For a future CAS it had been an ideal posting, and after such a fascinating tour he was a shade disappointed not to be given command of a front-line station. Instead he was despatched to Cranwell as the Unit Commander, responsible mainly for the aircraft and engineering support. These were the closing years of the Flight Cadet Scheme and while Craig was not personally involved in the change of policy he believed that the decision to fish in the university pool was correct. He stayed at Cranwell until mid-1970, and while much of the work was relatively routine he learnt a lot, not least about many of the issues affecting young officers and their training.

At this point, having served 19 years, he was selected for his first tour of overseas duty. With the main British withdrawal from the Far East almost complete, planning was starting for the much smaller force that the new Heath government had just agreed to retain in the area, and Craig was sent to head the tri-Service planning team at Headquarters Far East Command in Singapore. He stayed there barely a year, travelling much around the area, and helping ensure that Britain made her appropriate contribution under the Five-Power Defence Agreement. On his return home a proposal to appoint him Personal Staff Officer to CDS was quickly scotched, since he clearly needed experience of operational command, and in January 1972 he took over the RAF's largest station, Akrotiri, as an Air Commodore. Two squadrons of Vulcans, one of them his old squadron No 35, were based there in the low-level role, both earmarked for the Central Treaty Organisation, and not surprisingly Craig took much interest in their training, flying with them whenever he could. In addition there were resident Lightning, Hercules and Whirlwind squadrons, and these provided ample opportunities for him to extend his experience as a pilot. While this was a relatively quiet period in the history of Cyprus, Akrotiri was an exceedingly busy station, which had not only to support its own units but also to assist the United Nations peacekeeping force on the island and provide staging facilities on the route to the Far East; Craig found his two years there particularly rewarding.

The course at the Royal College of Defence Studies that followed in 1974 represented a complete change of pace, with a tour of African countries giving him an insight into a new part of the world, and he then spent a few months carrying out for Neil Cameron the staff study that led to the formation of the Administrative Branch. It was now time for another major appointment and he spent the next three years as ACAS (Operations). While there were no major crises, such matters as the firemen's strike, operations in Northern Ireland, and the deployment of Harriers to Belize demanded some of his attention, and the setting up of the Air Defence Ground Environment (the modernised complex of ground radars and command, control and communications systems) was an important preoccupation. However, his most valuable piece of work, he recalls, arose from the 1974 Defence Review, in which cuts in flying hours (and the cuts in support areas that would allegedly follow) were proposed as an economy measure. To counter this he and his staff had to establish the minimum amount of flying needed to maintain operational capability, a complex task entailing much work, and one of considerable long-term value.

Craig left the Ministry of Defence in 1978, returning to the bomber world as AOC 1 Group. For him it was still recognisable as the old Bomber Command, with the addition of the Buccaneer squadrons and the Victor tanker force, but the Vulcans were ageing and while the Tornado Training Establishment would soon be opened at Cottesmore, the introduction of the new aircraft into service still lay some years ahead. His chief concerns therefore lay with day-to-day operations, and he got around as much as possible, often flying the aircraft himself. Within less than two years, however, he was back at the centre of the RAF's affairs as VCAS, in time to be deeply concerned with the discussions surrounding John Nott's Defence Review. In his judgment it was not unreasonable to try to take a long view of how the defence vote should be shared, and with the defence of the home base seen as the first charge on an inevitably reduced budget it was right that the main cuts should fall on the maritime side. The Tornado programme was thus left intact, and he devoted much attention to the build-up of the strike squadrons, the way the later Air Defence Variant should be deployed, and the creation of the Operational Evaluation Unit at Boscombe Down.

It was during this time that the Falklands conflict occurred, and while much of the RAF work in the Ministry of Defence devolved upon Michael Beetham as CAS, and Kenneth Hayr as ACAS (Ops), Craig was always in touch with the main events and providing back-up when necessary. He was consulted on such matters as the use of the Vulcan and the shuffling of aircraft at the heavily overcrowded Ascension base, and assisted in some of the necessary liaison with other air forces. As he looks back he wishes the RAF's general contribution had been better publicised, but on the other hand he thinks there should have been tighter control over detailed military inform-ation whose release could have endangered our own forces.

Soon afterwards, in August 1982, he returned to Strike Command, this time as Commander-in-Chief, and for three years was responsible for the whole of the operational air force other than that stationed in Germany. Its tasks now included the commitment in the Falklands, whose air defence and air transport links were a major preoccupation. As CinC UK AIR his NATO roles also took much time, for the relationships with the other NATO commands, particularly the maritime, were constantly in need of adjustment and refinement. His three years at High Wycombe having brought him up to date on the RAF's multifarious activities, he was well set to return yet again to the Ministry of Defence in October 1985, this time as CAS.

The events of his term of office are too recent for any but the most general comment. He took over soon after the reorganisation of the Ministry of Defence by Michael Heseltine and thus had to manage with a smaller Air Staff and without a VCAS as his right-hand man. If in theory there should have been less work, this was not true in practice, and he was involved in several major government decisions. One of these was the termination of the Nimrod Airborne Early Warning programme and the ordering of the Boeing AWACS in its place; another was the agreement to proceed with the development of the European Fighter Aircraft. Then, after three years in office, he was appointed Chief of the Defence Staff in December 1988; he has thus found himself at the centre of the nation's defence counsels during the period in which the Soviet empire has shown signs of breaking up, with immense implications for the defence policy of the Western world, and not least the United Kingdom. The Kuwait crisis, too, has come his way. As historians look back in years to come, 1989 and 1990 will almost certainly be seen as the end of an era, and Sir David Craig will doubtless count himself privileged to have been able to play his part in these events at the culmination of his Royal Air Force career.

Appendix

The following summaries of each officer's record of service have been compiled largely from more detailed records held in the Air Historical Branch. They show the main promotion sequence, but not every switch between temporary, acting and substantive rank, and while all the important postings and major courses are given, many of the minor movements are omitted. Occasionally discrepancies exist between different types of record, and in such cases an element of judgement has had to be used. Nor has it been possible to obtain full information about those officers whose military careers began before the First World War, since many Army officers' records from this period were destroyed some years ago.

The list of honours and awards is limited to those received from British authorities. Some officers, particularly Trenchard and those who held high command during the Second World War, were also widely honoured by foreign governments.

Marshal of the Royal Air Force The Viscount Trenchard
GCB, OM, GCVO, DSO, DCL, LLD

Date of Birth: 3 February 1873

Date of Death: 10 February 1956

Service Honours and Awards:

Mentions in Despatches (25.8.05, 18.9.06, 22.6.15, 1.1.16, 15.6.16, 4.1.17, 11.12.17, 20.5.18, 10.4.19), DSO (18.9.06), CB (1.1.14), KCB (1.1.18), Baronet (30.12.19), GCB (1.1.24), Baron (of Wolfeton) (1.1.30), GCVO (26.7.35), Viscount (4.2.36), OM (1.1.51)

Promotions		Appointments
9. 9.93	2nd Lieutenant	Royal Scots Fusiliers
12. 8.96	Lieutenant	
28. 2.00	Captain	
22. 8.02	Brevet Major	
24.10.03	Temporary Lieutenant Colonel	Southern Nigerian Regiment
4.11.10		2nd Battalion, Royal Scots Fusiliers
17. 8.12		Central Flying School – Course
1.10.12		Central Flying School – Instructor
23. 9.13		Assistant Commandant, Central Flying School
7. 8.14		Officer Commanding, Military Wing, South Farnborough
18.11.14		Officer Commanding, HQ No 1 Wing, France
18. 1.15	Brevet Lieutenant Colonel	
3. 6.15	Brevet Colonel	
25. 8.15	Temporary Brigadier General	Officer Commanding, Royal Flying Corps, France
24. 3.16	Temporary Major General	General Officer Commanding, Royal Flying Corps, France
1. 1.17	Major General	
3. 1.18	Temporary Major General, RAF	
18. 1.18		Chief of the Air Staff
12. 4.18		Resigned
15. 5.18		Special Duty, Headquarters RAF France

Promotions		Appointments
15. 6.18		General Officer Commanding, Independent Force, France
26.10.18		Commander-in-Chief, Inter-Allied Air Force
20.11.18		Air Ministry
31. 3.19		Chief of the Air Staff
1. 8.19	Air Vice-Marshal	
11. 8.19	Air Marshal	
1. 4.22	Air Chief Marshal	
1. 1.27	Marshal of the Royal Air Force	
1. 1.30		Appointment relinquished

Major General The Right Honourable Sir Frederick Sykes

PC, GCSI, GCIE, GBE, KCB, CMG

Date of Birth: 23 July 1877
Date of Death: 30 September 1954
Service Honours and Awards:
Mentions in Despatches (19.10.14, 22.6.15, 6.1.16, 14.3.16), CMG (14.3.16), KCB
(1.1.19)

Promotions		*Appointments*
1900		Imperial Yeomanry Scouts, South Africa
		Lord Roberts's Bodyguard, South Africa
2.10.01	2nd Lieutenant	15th Hussars, India
		West African Regiment, Sierra Leone
1905	Captain	15th Hussars, India
1908		Staff College, Quetta
1910		South Africa
10.10	Major	Directorate of Operations, War Office
13. 5.12	Lieutenant Colonel RFC	OC Military Wing, RFC Farnborough
13. 8.14		Chief of Staff, HQ British Expeditionary Force
21.12.14	Temporary Colonel	Second-in-Command, RFC
26. 5.15		Placed at disposal of the Admiralty
24. 7.15	Temporary Captain, RNAS	OC Air Service Units, Dardanelles
14. 3.16	Colonel	Returned to Army service as AA & QMG, 4th Mounted Division, Colchester
1916	Brigadier-General	Deputy General of Organisation, War Office
11.17		Representative of AG and QMG on Supreme War Council
12. 4.18	Permanent Commission as Major General, RAF	Chief of the Air Staff
1. 4.19		Retirement

Marshal of the Royal Air Force Sir John Salmond

GCB, CMG, CVO, DSO, DCL, LLD

Date of Birth: 17 July 1881

Date of Death: 16 April 1968

Service Honours and Awards:

Mentions in Despatches (20.10.14, 9.12.14, 20.5,18, 31.12.18), DSO and Bar (18.2.15, 24.3.15), CMG (4.6.17), CVO (28.8.18), KCB (1.1.19), GCB (3.6.31)

Promotions		*Appointments*
8. 1.01	2nd Lieutenant	King's Own Royal Lancaster Regiment
5. 4.04	Lieutenant	
26. 6.10	Captain	
17. 8.12		Central Flying School
12.11.12	Flight Commander, RFC	Instructor, Central Flying School
31. 5.13	Squadron Commander, RFC	
30. 4.14		OC 3 Squadron, Farnborough
12. 8.14		OC 3 Squadron, France
13. 4.15	Wing Commander, RFC	Advanced Wing HQ, Farnborough
19. 8.15		OC 2 Wing, France
9. 3.16	Temporary Brigadier General	OC 6 Brigade
22. 6.17	Temporary Major General	OC Training Division
18.10.17		Director General of Military Aeronautics, War Office
18. 1.18		GOC Royal Flying Corps (in the Field)
1. 4.18	Major General, RAF	GOC Royal Air Force (in the Field)
7. 5.19		OC Rhine HQ
1. 8.19	Permanent Commission as Air Vice-Marshal	
19. 8.19		AOC South Area
1. 4.20		AOC Inland Area
1.10.22		AOC HQ Iraq
2. 6.23	Air Marshal	
1. 1.25		AOCinC Air Defence of Great Britain
1. 1.29	Air Chief Marshal	Air Member for Personnel
1. 1.30		Chief of the Air Staff
1. 1.33	Marshal of the Royal Air Force	
1. 4.33		Appointment relinquished

Marshal of the Royal Air Force Sir Edward Ellington
GCB, CMG, CBE

Date of Birth: 30 December 1877

Date of Death: 13 June 1967

Service Honours and Awards:

Mentions in Despatches (19.10.14, 1.1.16, 11.12.17), CMG (3.6.16), CB (1.1.19), CBE (3.6.19), (KCB (5.6.20), GCB (3.6.35)

Promotions		*Appointments*
1. 9.97	2nd Lieutenant	Royal Artillery
1. 9.00	Lieutenant	
27. 4.04	Captain	
08		War College, Portsmouth
24. 8.09		Staff Captain, War Office
9. 8.10		GSO 3, War Office
8. 5.13	Temporary Major	GSO 2, Directorate of Military Aeronautics, War Office
17.12.13	Squadron Commander, RFC	
5.10.14	Major, RA	DAQMG, HQ BEF, France
6. 3.15	Temporary Lieutenant Colonel	AA & QMG, 2nd Cavalry Division, BEF
22. 7.15	Temporary Colonel	GSO 1, 2nd Army, BEF
5. 2.16		GSO 1, War Office
14. 1.17	Temporary Brigadier-General	General Staff, 8th Army Corps, France
20.11.17		Deputy Director General of Military Aeronautics, War Office
18. 1.18		Director General of Military Aeronautics, War Office
10. 4.18	Temporary Major-General, RAF	Acting Controller-General of Equipment, Air Ministry
22. 8.18		Controller General of Equipment/ Director General of Supply and Research, Air Ministry
1. 8.19	Permanent Commision as Air Vice-Marshal	
1. 3.22		AOC HQ Middle East
5.11.23		AOC HQ India
19.11.26		AOC HQ Iraq

Promotions		Appointments
1. 1.29		AOCinC HQ Air Defence of Great Britain
1. 7.29	Air Marshal	
26. 9.31		Air Member for Personnel
1. 1.33	Air Chief Marshal	
22. 5.33		Chief of the Air Staff
1. 1.37	Marshal of the Royal Air Force	
1. 9.37		Inspector-General of the Royal Air Force
4. 4.40		Appointment relinquished

Marshal of the Royal Air Force The Lord Newall
GCB, OM, GCMG, CBE, AM

Date of Birth: 15 February 1886

Date of Death: 30 November 1963

Service Honours and Awards:

Albert Medal (19.5.16), Mentions in Despatches (15.5.16, 11.12.17, 1.1.19), CMG (1.1.19), CBE (3.6.19), CB (3.6.29), KCB (3.6.35), GCB (9.6.38), Order of Merit (1.11.40), GCMG (4.2.41), Baron (of Clifton-on-Dunsmoor) (13.6.46)

Promotions		Appointments
16. 8.05	2nd Lieutenant	Royal Warwickshire Regiment
16.11.07	Lieutenant	
16. 9.09		2nd Gurkha Rifles, India
5.13		Central Flying School, Upavon
7.11.13		Instructor, Indian Central Flying School, Sitapur
12. 9.14	Temporary Captain, RFC	1 Squadron
24. 3.15	Temporary Major, RFC	12 Squadron
10. 9.15		OC 12 Squadron, France
11. 2.16	Temporary Lieutenant-Colonel, RFC	OC 6 Wing
24.12.16		OC 9 Wing, France
11.10.17		OC 41 Wing
28.12.17	Temporary Brigadier-General, RFC	
22. 1.18		Commander, VIII Brigade, BEF
17. 3.19		Chief Staff Officer, SE Area
1. 8.19	Permanent Commission as Wing Commander, RAF	Deputy Director of Personnel, Air Ministry
8. 8.19	Group Captain	
24. 8.22		Deputy Commandant, 1 School of Technical Training, Halton
19. 1.25	Air Commodore	AOC Special Reserve and Auxiliary Air Force
1.12.25		League of Nations Disarmament Committee
12. 4.26		Director of Operations and Intelligence, and Deputy Chief of Air Staff

Promotions		Appointments
1. 1.30	Air Vice-Marshal	
6. 2.31		AOC Air Defence of Great Britain
7.10.31		AOC HQ Middle East
14. 1.35		Air Member for Supply and Organisation
1. 7.35	Air Marshal	
1. 4.37	Air Chief Marshal	
1. 9.37		Chief of the Air Staff
4.10.40	Marshal of the Royal Air Force	
24.10.40		Appointment relinquished

Air Chief Marshal The Lord Dowding

GCB, GCVO, CMG

Date of Birth: 24 April 1882

Date of Death: 15 February 1970

Service Honours and Awards:

Mention in Despatches (1.1.16), CMG (1.1.19), CB (2.1.28), KCB (3.6.33), GCVO (23.7.37), GCB (8.10.40), Baron (of Bentley Priory) (2.6.43)

Promotions		*Appointments*
18. 8.00	2nd Lieutenant, RA	
8. 5.02	Lieutenant, RA	
18. 8.13	Captain, RA	
5. 8.14	Flying Officer, RFC	Training, RFC
6.10.14		6 Squadron, France
18.11.14		GSO3, HQ RFC
4. 3.15	Temporary Major	OC 9 Squadron, France
26. 3.15		OC Wireless Experimental Establishment (9 Squadron), Brooklands
23. 7.15		OC 16 Squadron, France
22. 1.16	Temporary Lieutenant Colonel	7 Wing, Farnborough
18. 6.16		OC 9 Wing, France
1. 1.17	Temporary Colonel	Southern Group, Salisbury
23. 6.17	Temporary Brigadier-General	
1. 8.19	Permanent Commission as Group Captain	
18.10.19		OC 16 Group
29. 2.20		OC 1 Group, Kenley
1. 1.22	Air Commodore	
27. 2.23		Chief Staff Officer, HQ Inland Area, Uxbridge
19. 9.24		Chief Staff Officer, HQ Iraq Command
27. 5.26		Director of Training, Air Ministry
1. 1.29	Air Vice-Marshal	
7. 9.29		AOC Transjordan and Palestine
4. 1.30		AOC Fighting Area

Promotions		Appointments
1. 9.30		Air Member for Supply and Research
1. 1.33	Air Marshal	
14. 1.35		Air Member for Research and Development
14. 7.36		AOC in C Fighter Command
1. 1.37	Air Chief Marshal	
25.11.40		Appointment relinquished
18.12.40		Head of British Air Commission, Washington
1. 6.41		Appointment relinquished
14. 7.42		Last day of paid service

Marshal of the Royal Air Force The Viscount Portal of Hungerford

KG, GCB, OM, DSO, MC, DCL, LLD

Date of Birth: 21 May 1893

Date of Death: 22 April 1971

Service Honours and Awards:

Mentions in Despatches (9.12.14, 11.12.17, 31.12.18), MC (10.1.17), DSO (18.7.17) and Bar (26.7.18), CB (2.1.39), KCB (11.7.40), GCB (11.6.42), Baron (17.8.45), Viscount (1.1.46), OM (1.1.46), KG (3.12.46)

Promotions		Appointments
6. 8.14	Private, Royal Engineers	
26. 9.14	Temporary 2nd Lieutenant, RE	
5. 7.15		Observer, 3 Squadron, France
21.11.15	Flying Officer Observer, RFC	
10. 1.16		Castle Bromwich (flying instruction)
3. 5.16		60 Squadron, France
17. 7.16	Temporary Captain, RFC	Flight Commander, 3 Squadron, France
16. 6.17	Temporary Major, RFC	OC 16 Squadron, France
28. 6.18	Temporary Lieutenant-Colonel, RAF	OC 24 Wing
1. 8.19	Permanent Commission as Squadron Leader	
26. 4.19		OC 59 Wing, Cranwell
1. 6.19		HQ 12 Group, Cranwell
1.11.19		Chief Flying Instructor, Cranwell
3. 4.22		1 Course, RAF Staff College, Andover
4. 4.23		Directorate of Operations and Intelligence, Air Ministry
1. 7.25	Wing Commander	
11.10.26		Senior Officers' Course, Royal Naval College
11. 3.27		OC 7 Squadron, Bircham Newton
14. 1.29		Student, Imperial Defence College
16. 1.30		Special Duty, India
18. 4.30		Plans Branch, Air Ministry

Promotions		Appointments
1. 7.31	Group Captain	
20. 1.34		OC British Forces Aden
1. 1.35	Air Commodore	
14. 1.36		Directing Staff, Imperial Defence College
1. 7.37	Air Vice-Marshal	
1. 9.37		Director of Organisation, Air Ministry
1. 2.39		Air Member for Personnel
3. 9.39	Acting Air Marshal	
4. 4.40		AOCinC Bomber Command
25.10.40	Air Chief Marshal	Chief of the Air Staff
1. 1.44	Marshal of the Royal Air Force	
31.12.45		Appointment relinquished

Marshal of the Royal Air Force Sir Arthur Harris, Bt,

GCB, OBE, AFC, LLD

Date of Birth: 13 April 1892

Date of Death: 5 April 1984

Service Honours and Awards:

AFC (2.11.18), OBE (3.6.27), Mentions in Despatches (15.9.39, 1.1.41), CB (11.7.40), KCB (11.6.42), GCB (14.6.45), Baronet (1.1.53)

Promotions		*Appointments*
1.10.15		Brooklands
6.11.15	2nd Lieutenant, RFC	
28.11.15		Central Flying School
29. 1.16	Flying Officer, RFC	11 Squadron
15. 2.16		19 Squadron
24. 3.16	Temporary Captain	
18. 4.16		39 Squadron, Northolt
14. 7.16		38 Squadron, Castle Bromwich
27. 9.16		70 Squadron, France
2. 3.17		51 Squadron, Wye
18. 6.17		45 Squadron, France
1. 1.18	Temporary Major	OC 191 Training Squadron, Marham
8. 6.18		OC 44 Squadron, France
19.12.18		OC 50 Squadron
1. 8.19	Permanent Commission as Squadron Leader	
29. 7.19		2 Group
26. 4.20		OC 3 Flying Training School
26. 1.21		OC 21 Squadron, India
28. 7.22		Group Headquarters, Basrah
20.11.22		OC 45 Squadron, Iraq
25. 5.25		OC 58 Squadron, Worthy Down
1. 7.27	Wing Commander	
21. 1.28		Student, Army Staff College, Camberley
3. 1.30		Senior Staff Officer, AOC Middle East Command
3.10.32		Flying Boat Pilots' Course, Calshot

Promotions		Appointments
21. 3.33		OC 210 Squadron
11. 7.33		Deputy Director of Operations and Intelligence, Air Ministry
3. 4.34		Deputy Director of Plans, Air Ministry
1. 7.35	Group Captain	
12. 6.37	Air Commodore	AOC 4 Group
1. 7.38		AOC HQ Palestine and Transjordan
1. 7.39	Air Vice-Marshal	
11. 9.39		AOC 5 Group
25.11.40		Deputy Chief of Air Staff
27. 5.41	Air Marshal (Acting)	Head of British Air Staff, Washington
22. 2.42		AOCinC Bomber Command
18. 3.43	Air Chief Marshal (Acting)	
15. 9.45		Appointment relinquished
1. 1.46	Marshal of the Royal Air Force	

Marshal of the Royal Air Force The Lord Douglas of Kirtleside

GCB, MC, DFC, DL

Date of Birth: 23 December 1893

Date of Death: 29 October 1969

Service Honours and Awards:

Mentions in Despatches (1.1.16, 20.5.18, 31.12.18), MC (14.1.16), DFC (8.2.19), CB (11.7.40), KCB (1.7.41), GCB (1.1.46), Baron (1.1.48)

Promotions		Appointments
15. 8.14	2nd Lieutenant	Royal Field Artillery
7. 1.15		2 Squadron, France (Observer)
10. 6.15	Lieutenant	Shoreham/14 Squadron (Pilot training)
16. 8.15	Flying Officer, RFC	8 Squadron, France
10. 1.16	Temporary Captain, RFC	18 Squadron
15. 4.16	Temporary Major, RFC	OC 43 Squadron, UK and France
10. 8.17		OC 84 Squadron, France
20.11.18	Acting Lieutenant Colonel, RAF	OC 59 Wing
21. 4.19	Unemployed List	–
25. 3.20	Permanent Commission as Squadron Leader	HQ 1 Group, Kenley
4. 4.21		School of Technical Training
22. 7.21		CFI, 6 Flying Training School, Manston
3. 4.22		No 1 Course, RAF Staff College
4. 4.23		Directorate of Training, Air Ministry
1. 1.25	Wing Commander	
17. 1.27		Student, Imperial Defence College
6. 1.28		OC RAF North Weald
16. 8.29		Air Staff duties, Middle East
27. 6.32	Group Captain	Instructor, Imperial Defence College
1. 1.36	Air Commodore	Director of Staff Duties, Air Ministry
17. 2.38	Air Vice-Marshal	Assistant Chief of Air Staff
22. 4.40		Deputy Chief of Air Staff
25.11.40	Air Marshal	AOCinC Fighter Command

Promotions		Appointments
1. 7.42	Air Chief Marshal (Temporary)	
11. 1.43		AOCinC RAF Middle East
20. 1.44		AOCinC Coastal Command
15. 7.45		AOCinC Air Division, Control Commission for Germany
1. 1.46	Marshal of the Royal Air Force	
1. 5.46		CinC British Armed Forces of Occupation, United Kingdom Member of the Control Commission and Military Governor of the British Zone of Germany
1.11.47		Appointment relinquished

Marshal of the Royal Air Force The Lord Tedder

GCB, DCL, LLD, BA

Date of Birth: 11 July 1890

Date of Death: 3 June 1967

Service Honours and Awards:

Mentions in Despatches (22.1.19, 5.6.19), CB (1.2.37), KCB (1.1.42), Commendation (3.6.42), GCB (27.11.42), Baron (of Glenguin) (1.1.46)

Promotions		*Appointments*
2. 9.13	2nd Lieutenant	Dorset Regiment
10. 1.15	Lieutenant	
15. 1.16		1 School of Aeronautics
21. 3.16	Captain	
27. 4.16		Civil Flying School
16. 6.16	Flying Officer, RFC	25 Squadron, France
9. 8.16	Temporary Captain, RFC	Flight Commander, 25 Squadron
1. 1.17	Temporary Major, RFC	OC 70 Squadron, France
25. 6.17		OC 67 Training Squadron
24. 6.18	Acting Lieutenant Colonel, RAF	OC 38 Training Wing, Middle East
20. 5.19	Major, RAF	OC 274 Squadron
1. 8.19	Permanent Commission as Squadron Leader	
18.11.21		OC 207 Squadron
24. 9.23		Course at Naval Staff College
1. 1.24	Wing Commander	
27.11.24		OC 2 Flying Training School, Digby
1. 1.27		Directorate of Training, Air Ministry
16. 1.28		Student, Imperial Defence College
3. 1.29		Directing Staff, RAF Staff College
1. 1.31	Group Captain	
26. 1.32		OC Air Armament School, Eastchurch
4. 4.34		Director of Training, Air Ministry
1. 7.34	Air Commodore	
11.11.36		AOC HQ Far East
1. 7.37	Air Vice-Marshal	

Promotions		Appointments
20. 7.38		Director General of Research and Development, Air Ministry
1. 8.40		Deputy Air Member of Development and Production, Ministry of Aircraft Production
29.11.40	Air Marshal (Acting)	Deputy AOCinC, RAF Middle East
1. 6.41	Air Marshal	AOCinC, RAF Middle East
1. 7.42	Air Chief Marshal (Temporary)	
17. 2.43		Commander in Chief, Mediterranean Allied Air Forces
17. 1.44		Air Commander-in-Chief and Deputy Supreme Allied Commander, Allied Expeditionary Force
12. 9.45	Marshal of the Royal Air Force	
1. 1.46		Chief of the Air Staff
31.12.49		Appointment relinquished
1. 4.50		Chairman of British Joint-Services Mission, Washington, and British Representative on Standing Group of the NATO Military Organisation
30. 5.41		Appointment relinquished

Marshal of the Royal Air Force Sir John Slessor
GCB, DSO, MC

Date of Birth: 3 June 1897
Date of Death: 12 July 1979
Service Honours and Awards:
Mentions in Despatches (25.10.16, 18.2.38), MC (1.1.17), DSO (10.12.37), CB (1.1.42), KCB (2.6.43), GCB (10.6.48)

Promotions		*Appointments*
14. 6.15		Brooklands
6. 7.15	2nd Lieutenant RFC	
19. 8.15		Gosport
15. 9.15	Flying Officer RFC	23 Squadron, Suttons Farm
4.11.15		17 Squadron, Middle East
20. 9.16		4 Squadron, Northolt
1.12.16	Temporary Captain, RFC	
1. 2.17		58 Squadron, France
2. 5.17		5 Squadron, France
15. 2.18		HQ 28 Wing (Artillery and Infantry Co-operation Officer)
3. 7.18	Temporary Major, RAF	Central Flying School
14. 5.19		14 Squadron
17. 7.19		201 Squadron
21. 8.19	Unemployed List	–
24. 2.20	Permanent Commission as Flight Lieutenant	1 Flying Training School, Netheravon
4. 5.21		20 Squadron, India
25. 1.23		Directorate of Staff Duties, Air Ministry
5. 5.24		3 Course, RAF Staff College
1. 1.25	Squadron Leader	
4. 5.25		OC 4 Squadron, Farnborough
1.10.28		Directorate of Operations and Intelligence, Air Ministry
1.10.30		School of Army Co-operation
21. 1.31		RAF Instructor, Army Staff College Camberley

Promotions		Appointments
1. 1.32	Wing Commander	
13. 3.35		OC 3 Wing, India
17. 5.37	Group Captain	Deputy Director of Plans, Air Ministry
22.12.38		Director of Plans, Air Ministry
1. 9.39	Air Commodore	
21.10.40		Special Duty in the USA
10. 1.41	Air Vice-Marshal	
12. 5.41		AOC 5 Group
6. 4.42		Assistant Chief of Air Staff (Policy)
5. 2.43	Air Marshal (Acting)	AOCinC Coastal Command
14. 1.44		Deputy Air CinC, Mediterranean Allied Air Forces, and CinC RAF Mediterranean and Middle East
5. 4.45		Air Member for Personnel
1. 1.46	Air Chief Marshal	
1. 1.48		Commandant, Imperial Defence College
1. 1.50		Chief of the Air Staff
8. 6.50	Marshal of the Royal Air Force	
31.12.52		Appointment relinquished

Marshal of the Royal Air Force Sir William Dickson

GCB, KBE, DSO, AFC

Date of Birth: 24 September 1898

Date of Death: 12 September 1987

Service Honours and Awards:

Mentions in Despatches (1.10.17, 1.1.19, 26.6.31), DSO (21.9.18), AFC (3.6.22), OBE (4.6.34), CB (11.6.42), CBE (5.7.45), KBE (1.1.46), KCB (1.1.52), GCB (1.1.53)

Promotions		*Appointments*
8.10.16	Flight Officer RNAS (probation)	Windermere/Calshot
12. 4.17	Flight Sub-Lieutenant (temporary)	Isle of Grain
2. 8.17		HMS FURIOUS
31.12.17	Flight Lieutenant (temporary)	
1. 4.18	Lieutenant (Flying Officer) RAF	
23.10.18		HMS REVENGE
8. 4.19		HMS QUEEN ELIZABETH
1. 8.19	Permanent Commission	
25. 3.20		Gosport
3. 1.21		HMS ARGUS
19. 5.21		Experimental Section, Royal Aircraft Establishment, Farnborough
30. 6.22	Flight Lieutenant	
20. 3.23		Air Ministry
19. 7.26		56 Squadron, Biggin Hill
19. 9.27		6 Course, RAF Staff College Andover
12. 2.29		No 1 Indian Wing
4. 4.30		Air Staff, HQ India
5.11.30	Squadron Leader	
19. 9.34		Air Staff, HQ Western Area
14. 1.35		OC 25 Squadron, Hawkinge
2. 3.36	Wing Commander	Directing Staff, RAF Staff College
17. 1.39		Imperial Defence College
3. 7.39		Directorate of Plans, Air Ministry
1. 1.40	Group Captain (Temporary)	

Promotions		Appointments
1. 3.41		Director of Plans, Air Ministry
30. 4.41	Air Commodore (Acting)	
17. 5.42		SASO 9 Group, Preston
26. 6.42	Air Vice-Marshal (Acting)	AOC 9 Group
2.11.42		AOC 10 Group, Rudloe Manor
21. 3.43		AOC 83 Group
4. 4.44		AOC Desert Air Force, Italy
21.12.44		Assistant Chief of Air Staff (Policy)
1. 6.46	Air Marshal (Acting)	Vice Chief of Air Staff
1. 3.48		AOCinC Mediterranean and Middle East, Ismailia
2. 3.50		Air Member for Supply and Organisation
8. 1.51	Air Chief Marshal	
1. 1.53		Chief of the Air Staff
1. 6.54	Marshal of the Royal Air Force	
1. 1.56		Chairman, Chiefs of Staff Committee
1. 1.59		Chief of the Defence Staff
16. 7.59		Appointment relinquished

Marshal of the Royal Air Force Sir Dermot Boyle

GCB, KCVO, KBE, AFC

Date of Birth: 2 October 1904

Service Honours and Awards:

AFC (8.6.39), Mentions in Despatches (1.1.41, 24.9.41, 2.6.43), CBE (1.1.45), CB (1.1.46), KBE (1.1.53), KCVO (16.7.53), GCB (1.1.57)

Promotions		*Appointments*
14. 9.22	Flight Cadet	RAF College Cranwell
31. 7.24	Pilot Officer (Permanent Commission)	17 Squadron, Hawkinge
15.12.25		1 Squadron, Iraq
31. 1.26	Flying Officer	
1.11.26		6 Squadron, Iraq
12. 3.27		Central Flying School
13.11.29	Flight Lieutenant	
16. 1.30		RAF College Cranwell
5. 1.31		601 Squadron, Hendon
7. 4.33		Personnel Staff, Headquarters India
21. 1.36		14 Course, RAF Staff College Andover
1.10.36	Squadron Leader	
2. 1.37		OC 83 Squadron, Turnhouse
19. 7.37		Chief Flying Instructor, RAF College Cranwell
21.11.39	Wing Commander	Headquarters, Advanced Air Striking Force, France
28. 6.40		Operations Staff, Headquarters Bomber Command
21.11.40		OC 83 Squadron, Scampton
17. 2.41		Assistant Secretary, Committee of Imperial Defence
1.12.41	Group Captain (Temporary)	
17. 1.42		OC RAF Stradishall
17. 5.43	Air Commodore (Acting)	SASO 83 Group
26. 4.45	Air Vice-Marshal (Acting)	AOC 85 Group
20. 7.45		AOC 11 Group
2. 4.46	Air Commodore	Imperial Defence College

Promotions		Appointments
2. 1.47		Assistant Commandant, RAF Staff College Bracknell
26. 7.48	Air Vice-Marshal (Acting)	Director General of Personnel (1) Air Ministry
4. 7.49	Air Vice-Marshal	Director General of Manning, Air Ministry
5. 4.51		AOC 1 Group
7. 4.53	Air Marshal	AOCinC Fighter Command
1. 1.56	Air Chief Marshal	Chief of the Air Staff
1. 1.58	Marshal of the Royal Air Force	
1. 1.60		Appointment relinquished

Marshal of the Royal Air Force Sir Thomas Pike

GCB, CBE, DFC

Date of Birth: 29 June 1906

Date of Death: 3 June 1983

Service Honours and Awards:

DFC (13.5.41), Bar to DFC (30.5.41), Mention in Despatches (2.6.43), CBE (8.6.44), CB (1.1.46), KCB (9.6.55), GCB (31.12.60)

Promotions		Appointments
17. 1.24	Flight Cadet	RAF College Cranwell
16.12.25	Pilot Officer (Permanent Commission)	56 Squadron, Biggin Hill/North Weald
16. 6.27	Flying Officer	
2.10.28		Central Flying School, Wittering
19.12.28		Instructor, 5 Flying Training School, Sealand
6. 5.29		Instructor, Central Flying School
5. 8.30	Flight Lieutenant	Long Engineering Course, Henlow
1.10.32		Middle East Depot, Aboukir
13.11.34		Instructor, 4 Flying Training School, Abu Sueir
19. 1.37	Squadron Leader	15 Course, RAF Staff College, Andover
1. 1.38		Chief Flying Instructor, 10 Flying Training School, Ternhill
14. 2.39		Directorate of Organisation, Air Ministry
4. 1.40	Wing Commander (Acting)	
4. 2.41		OC 219 Squadron, Tangmere
29. 9.41	Group Captain (Acting)	Operations Staff, HQ 11 Group
2. 2.42		OC RAF North Weald
5. 8.42		Senior Officer Administration, HQ 11 Group
16. 5.43		OC 1 Mobile Operations Room, Mediterranean Allied Air Forces
21. 2.44	Air Commodore (Acting)	SASO, HQ Desert Air Force
23. 6.45		OC 1 Officers' Advanced Training School, Cranwell/Digby

Promotions		Appointments
12.10.46		Director of Operational Requirements, Air Ministry
1. 7.47	Air Commodore	
11. 1.49		Imperial Defence College
9. 1.50	Air Vice-Marshal (Acting)	AOC 11 Group, Hillingdon
1. 7.50	Air Vice-Marshal	
21. 7.51		Deputy Chief of Staff, Operations, HQ Allied Air Forces Central Europe
12. 6.53		Assistant Chief of Air Staff (Policy)
9.11.53	Air Marshal (Acting)	Deputy Chief of Air Staff
1. 1.55	Air Marshal	
8. 8.56		AOCinC Fighter Command
1.11.57	Air Chief Marshal	
1. 1.60		Chief of the Air Staff
6. 4.62	Marshal of the Royal Air Force	
1. 9.63		Appointment relinquished
1. 1.64		Deputy Supreme Allied Commander Europe
1. 3.67		Appointment relinquished

Marshal of the Royal Air Force the Lord Elworthy

KG, GCB, CBE, DSO, LVO, DFC, AFC, MA

Date of Birth: 23 March 1911

Service Honours and Awards:

AFC (1.1.41), DFC (7.3.41), DSO (22.4.41), Mentions in Despatches (24.9.41, 1.1.43, 14.1.44), CBE (1.1.46), MVO (16.7.53), CB (1.1.60), KCB (31.12.60), GCB (1.1.62), Baron (of Timaru) (9.5.72)

Promotions		Appointments
14. 8.33	Pilot Officer on probation	Reserve of Air Force Officers
14. 8.34	Pilot Officer	
15. 1.35		600 Squadron, Auxiliary Air Force
28.10.35		15 Squadron, Abingdon
3. 3.36	Permanent Commission	
3. 9.36	Flying Officer	
22.11.37		Personal Assistant to AOCinC Bomber Command, Uxbridge
3. 9.38	Flight Lieutenant	
11. 1.39		108 Squadron, Bassingbourn – Bicester
6. 9.39	Squadron Leader (Acting)	
8. 4.40		Chief Flying Instructor, 13 Operational Training Unit, Bicester
26. 8.40		82 Squadron, Watton
14.12.40	Wing Commander (Acting)	OC 82 Squadron
6. 5.41		Operations Room, HQ 2 Group
20.10.41		Operations Room, Bomber Command, High Wycombe
9. 5.42	Group Captain (Acting)	Group Captain Operations, Bomber Command
16. 4.43		OC RAF Waddington
4. 4.44		Air Staff, Deputy Supreme Commander
22.8.44	Air Commodore (Acting)	SASO 5 Group
1.12.45	Group Captain (Acting)	Central Bombing Establishment, Marham
6. 3.47		SASO 2 (Indian) Group
1.11.47		OC Royal Pakistan Air Force Station, Drigh Road

Promotions		Appointments
23. 5.49	Wing Commander	5 Course, Joint Services Staff College Latimer
1. 7.49	Group Captain	
19.12.49		Deputy Director of Personnel 2, Air Ministry
5.12.51		OC RAF Tangmere
13. 3.53		OC RAF Odiham
1.12.53	Air Commodore (Acting)	Commander, Metropolitan Sector, North Weald
9. 1.56	Air Commodore	Imperial Defence College
1. 1.57	Air Vice-Marshal (Acting)	Commandant, RAF Staff College, Bracknell
1. 7.57	Air Vice-Marshal	
15.11.59	Air Marshal (Acting)	Deputy Chief of Air Staff
28. 7.60	Air Marshal	Commander-in-Chief British Forces Aden Peninsula/Middle East Command
1. 9.62	Air Chief Marshal	
1. 9.63		Chief of the Air Staff
1. 4.67	Marshal of the Royal Air Force	
4. 8.67		Chief of the Defence Staff
8. 4.71		Appointment relinquished

Marshal of the Royal Air Force Sir John Grandy

GCB, GCVO, KBE, DSO

Date of Birth: 8 February 1913

Service Honours and Awards:

Mentions in Despatches (1.1.43, 1.1.45), DSO (19.10.45), CB (31.5.56), KBE (10.6.61), KCB (13.6.64), GCB (1.1.67), GCVO (1.1.88)

Promotions		Appointments
11. 9.31	Pilot Officer on Probation	RAF Depot
26. 9.31		5 Flying Training School, Sealand
29. 8.32		54 (Fighter) Squadron, Hornchurch
11. 9.32	Pilot Officer	
11. 6.33	Flying Officer	
15. 4.35		604 (County of Middlesex) Squadron, Hendon
13. 1.36		Central Flying School
30. 3.36		9 Flying Training School, Thornaby
11. 6.36	Flight Lieutenant	
11. 9.36	Permanent Commission	
5. 1.37		University of London Air Squadron
1. 2.39	Squadron Leader	
13. 2.39		13 Flying Training School, Drem
6.11.39		Central Gunnery School
14. 4.40		OC 219 Squadron, Catterick
16. 5.40		OC 249 Squadron, Church Fenton – Boscombe Down – North Weald
6.12.40		HQ Fighter Command
22. 2.41		52 Operational Training Unit
1. 3.41	Wing Commander (Temporary)	
23.11.41		OC Flying, Coltishall
12. 2.42	Group Captain (Acting)	OC RAF Duxford
1. 2.43		OC 210 Air Defence Group, North Africa
19. 9.43		OC 73 Operational Training Unit, Abu Sueir – Fayid
1. 7.44	Group Captain (Temporary)	

Promotions		Appointments
3. 2.45		OC 341 Wing, Air Command South-East Asia
15. 9.45		SASO HQ 232 Group
2. 5.46		17 Staff Course, Army Staff College, Camberley
14.12.46		Deputy Director of Training, Air Ministry
8 1.49		Air Attache, Brussels
1. 1.50	Group Captain	
13.11.50		HQ Northern Sector, Fighter Command
19. 5.52		Operations Staff, HQ Fighter Command
11. 5.53	Air Commodore (Acting)	
10.12.54		Commandant, Central Fighter Establishment
1. 1.56	Air Commodore	
8. 1.57		Imperial Defence College
2. 9.57		Commander Task Force Grapple
9.11.57	Air Vice-Marshal (Acting)	
1. 7.58	Air Vice-Marshal	
17.10.58		ACAS (Ops) Air Ministry
7. 1.61	Air Marshal (Acting)	CinC RAF Germany and Commander 2 ATAF
1. 1.62	Air Marshal	
1. 9.63		AOCinC Bomber Command
1. 4.65	Air Chief Marshal	
28. 5.65		CinC Far East Command
1. 4.67		Chief of the Air Staff
1. 4.71	Marshal of the Royal Air Force	Appointment relinquished

Marshal of the Royal Air Force Sir Denis Spotswood

GCB, CBE, DSO, DFC

Date of Birth: 26 September 1916

Service Honours and Awards:

Mentions in Despatches (24.9.41 and 2.6.43), DFC (10.11.42), DSO (28.9.43), CBE (1.1.46), CB (31.12.60), KCB (11.6.66), GCB (1.1.71)

Promotions		Appointments
3. 2.36		Civil Flying School, Reading
30. 3.36	Pilot Officer on Probation	
18. 4.36		6 Flying Training School, Netheravon
10. 1.37		220 (General Reconnaissance) Squadron
3. 2.37	Pilot Officer	
8. 2.37		Courses (206 Sqn, School of Air Navigation, and Calshot)
8.10.37		201 Squadron, Calshot
26. 2.38		209 Squadron, Felixstowe – Invergordon – Oban – Pembroke Dock – Stranraer – Lough Erne
3. 9.38	Flying Officer	
2. 3.39	Flight Lieutenant (Acting)	
21. 7.41	Squadron Leader (Acting)	6 Operational Training Unit
18. 4.42	Wing Commander (Acting)	OC 500 Squadron, Stornoway – St Eval – Tafaroui – Blida
22. 4.43		Air Tactics 3, Air Ministry
30. 8.43		10 (War) Course, RAF Staff College Bulstrode
11. 2.44	Group Captain (Acting)	Plans Branch, Air Command South-East Asia, Delhi – Ceylon
1. 9.45	Permanent Commission	
12. 2.46	Wing Commander (Temporary)	Directing Staff, RAF Staff College Bracknell
1. 7.47	Wing Commander	
19.12.47		OC RAF Horsham St Faith
30. 1.48		OC RAF Coltishall
13. 3.50		Directing Staff, Imperial Defence College

Promotions		Appointments
21. 6.52	Group Captain (Acting)	Tactical Operations Plans Branch, HQ USAF, Washington
1. 1.54	Group Captain	
13. 8.54		OC RAF Linton-on-Ouse
15.10.56		Deputy Director of Plans, Air Ministry
26. 8.58	Air Commodore (Acting)	AOC and Commandant, RAF College, Cranwell
1. 1.60	Air Commodore	
5. 6.61	Air Vice-Marshal	Assistant Chief of Staff, Air Defence Division, SHAPE
28.11.63		Chairman of Pathfinder Study, Air Ministry
26. 5.64		Series of flying refresher courses
5. 8.64		AOC 3 Group, Mildenhall
6.12.65	Air Marshal	Commander-in-Chief RAF Germany
26. 8.68	Air Chief Marshal	AOCinC Strike Command
1. 4.71		Chief of the Air Staff
31. 3.74	Marshal of the Royal Air Force	Appointment relinquished

Marshal of the Royal Air Force Sir Andrew Humphrey

GCB, OBE, DFC, AFC

Date of Birth: 10 January 1921

Date of Death: 24 January 1977

Service Honours and Awards:

DFC (30.5.41), AFC (1.1.43), Bar to AFC (1.1.45), OBE (1.1.51), Second Bar to AFC (9.6.55), CB (13.6.59), Mention in Despatches (23.1.68), KCB (8.6.68), GCB (1.1.74)

Promotions		*Appointments*
12. 1.39	Flight Cadet	RAF College Cranwell
1. 5.40	Pilot Officer (Permanent Commission)	
4. 5.40		9 Bombing and Gunnery School
16. 9.40		266 Squadron, Wittering
1. 5.41	Flying Officer	
19. 7.41		452 Squadron, Kenley
17. 8.41	Flight Lieutenant (Acting)	58 Operational Training Unit, Grangemouth
3. 3.42		Flight Commander, 175 Squadron, Warmwell
18. 7.42		58 Operational Training Unit, Grangemouth
3. 1.43		Specialised Low Attack Instructors' School, Milfield
12. 4.43		RAF Middle East – Specialised Low Attack Instructor
19. 7.43		6 Squadron, Tunisia and Canal Zone
15.10.43	Squadron Leader (Acting)	
10. 1.44		RAF Shallufa, Canal Zone
29. 6.44		RAF Nicosia, Cyprus
20.11.44	Wing Commander (Acting)	RAF Ranchi, India
4. 8.45		HQ British Air Forces South East Asia, New Delhi
21. 8.46	Squadron Leader	HQ 106 Group, RAF Benson
1. 9.48		Flight Commander, 82 Squadron, Africa
28. 2.51		RAF Flying College, Manby
1. 7.51	Wing Commander	

Promotions		Appointments
16. 2.53		Senior Instructor, RAF Flying College
10. 1.55		45 Course, RAF Staff College Bracknell
1. 2.56		OR 20, Air Ministry
18. 1.57	Group Captain	DDOR 4, Air Ministry
10. 2.59		OC RAF Akrotiri, Cyprus
8. 1.62		Imperial Defence College
1. 7.62	Air Commodore	
26.11.62		Director of Joint Plans, Air Ministry
1. 4.64		Director of Defence Plans (Air), Ministry of Defence
1.12.64		Special Duties, Ministry of Defence, followed by refresher flying courses
1. 1.65	Air Vice-Marshal	
14.12.65		AOC Air Forces Middle East, Aden
30.11.67	Air Marshal	Air Member for Personnel
1.12.70	Air Chief Marshal	
5. 1.71		AOCinC, Strike Command
1. 4.74		Chief of the Air Staff
6. 8.76	Marshal of the Royal Air Force	Appointment relinquished
24.10.76		Chief of the Defence Staff
24. 1.77		Died in post

Marshal of the Royal Air Force the Lord Cameron of Balhousie

KT, GCB, CBE, DSO, DFC, AE, LLD

Date of Birth: 8 July 1920

Date of Death: 30 January 1985

Service Honours and Awards:

Mention in Despatches (2.6.43), DFC (21.11.44), DSO (2.10.45), CBE (10.6.67), CB (1.1.71), KCB (1.1.75), GCB (12.6.76), Baron (14.3.83)

Promotions		*Appointments*
13. 5.39	Sgt Pilot (under training)	Perth (part-time)
1. 9.39		Mobilised
1.10.39		3 Initial Training Wing, Hastings
26. 3.40		15 Elementary Flying Training School, Redhill
8. 6.40		8 Service Flying Training School, Montrose
31. 8.40	Sgt Pilot	5 Operational Training Unit, Aston Down
26. 9.40		1 Squadron, Wittering
15.10.40		17 Squadron, Martlesham Heath
31. 7.41	Pilot Officer	134 Squadron, Murmansk – Northern Ireland
4.12.41	Flight Lieutenant (Acting)	
28. 8.42		213 Squadron, North Africa
31. 3.43	Squadron Leader (Acting)	335 Squadron, Royal Hellenic Air Force, Egypt
5.10.43		Operations Staff, HQ 224 Group, India
1. 2.44		OC 258 Squadron, India and Burma
1. 9.45	Permanent Commission	
13.10.45		School of Air Support, Old Sarum
14. 4.48		Liaison Officer, British Army of the Rhine
25.10.48	Flight Lieutenant	6 Course, RAF Staff College Andover
22. 5.49	Squadron Leader (Acting)	Directorate of Organisation (04), Air Ministry
1. 1.50	Squadron Leader	
31. 1.52		Air Ministry Selection Board, London

Promotions		Appointments
8.12.53	Wing Commander (Acting)	Directing Staff, RAF Staff College Bracknell
1. 1.56	Wing Commander	
26. 8.56		OC University of London Air Squadron, Kenley
10.11.58		Personal Staff Officer to Chief of the Air Staff
1. 7.60	Group Captain	
24.10.60		OC RAF Abingdon
8. 1.63		Imperial Defence College
20.12.63		Personal Staff Officer to Deputy Supreme Allied Commander Europe
1. 7.64	Air Commodore	
15. 2.65		RAF College Cranwell (Assistant Commandant (Cadets) from 1.5.65)
26. 9.66		RAF Member of Programme Evaluation Group, Ministry of Defence
1. 2.68	Air Vice-Marshal	Assistant Chief of Defence Staff (Policy)
1. 8.70		SASO Air Support Command, Upavon
1. 9.72		Chief of Staff, 46 Group, Upavon
4.12.72		Deputy Commander, RAF Germany
24.11.73	Air Marshal	AOC 46 Group
5.10.74		Air Member for Personnel
1.11.75	Air Chief Marshal	
7. 8.76		Chief of the Air Staff
31. 7.77	Marshal of the Royal Air Force	
31. 8.77		Chief of the Defence Staff
1. 9.79		Appointment relinquished

Marshal of the Royal Air Force Sir Michael Beetham

GCB, CBE, DFC, AFC

Date of Birth: 17 May 1923

Service Honours and Awards:

DFC (6.6.44), King's Commendation (1.1.52), AFC (1.1.60), CBE (1.1.67), GCB (1.1.78)

Promotions		Appointments
6.10.41	U/T Pilot	Initial training
9. 1.42		Pilot training in USA
13.12.42	Pilot Officer	
6. 4.43		18 Advanced Flying Unit
1. 6.43		14 Operational Training Unit
13. 6.43	Flying Officer	
8. 9.43		1654 Operational Conversion Unit
15. 1.44	Flight Lieutenant (Acting)	50 Squadron, Skellingthorpe
14. 6.44		5 Lancaster Finishing School
30. 3.45		57 Squadron, East Kirkby
24. 6.45	Squadron Leader (Acting)	Flight Commander, 57 Squadron
1. 9.45	Permanent Commission	
24.11.45		Flight Commander, 35 Squadron, Graveley
24. 2.47	Flight Lieutenant	Personnel Staff, Headquarters Bomber Command
26. 5.49		82 Squadron, Africa
6.11.51		205 Advanced Flying School
1. 1.52	Squadron Leader	
28. 4.52		10 Course, RAF Staff College, Andover
15. 4.53		Staff of DDOR 1, Air Ministry
7. 5.56		Task Force, Operation Buffalo
10. 2.57		3 All-weather Jet Squadron, Manby
24. 4.57		231 Operational Conversion Unit
22. 7.57		RAF Gaydon (Valiant course)
1. 1.58	Wing Commander	
10. 2.58		OC 214 Squadron, Marham

Promotions		Appointments
7. 6.60		Operations Staff, Headquarters 3 Group, Mildenhall
4.10.61	Group Captain	Training Staff, Headquarters Bomber Command
9. 7.62		Operations Staff, Headquarters Bomber Command
23.10.64		OC RAF Khormaksar, Aden
1. 7.66	Air Commodore	
10. 1.67		Imperial Defence College
4. 1.68		Director of Operational Requirements, Ministry of Defence
11.11.68		Director of Strike Operations, Ministry of Defence
27. 9.70	Air Vice-Marshal	Commandant, RAF Staff College, Bracknell
14. 8.72		Assistant Chief of Staff (Plans & Policy), SHAPE, Belgium
7.6.75	Air Marshal	Deputy Commander-in-Chief, Strike Command
19. 1.76		Commander 2nd Allied Tactical Air Force and Commander-in-Chief RAF Germany
21. 5.77	Air Chief Marshal	
1. 8.77		Chief of the Air Staff
14.10.82	Marshal of the Royal Air Force	Appointment relinquished

Marshal of the Royal Air Force Sir Keith Williamson

GCB, AFC

Date of Birth: 25 February 1928

Service Honours and Awards:

AFC (8.6.68), KCB (1.1.79), GCB (12.6.82)

Promotions		Appointments
13. 2.45	Aircraft Apprentice	Radio School, Cranwell
29. 4.48	Flight Cadet	RAF College, Cranwell
13.12.50	Pilot Officer (Permanent Commission)	
16. 1.51		203 Advanced Flying School, Driffield
15. 5.51		229 Operational Conversion Unit
27. 7.51		112 Squadron, Fassberg – Jever
13.12.51	Flying Officer	
25. 5.53		Far East Air Force – Korea
13. 6.53	Flight Lieutenant	
17. 2.54		ADC to AOCinC Home Command
22. 4.56		7 Flying Training School, Valley
27. 5.56		229 Operational Conversion Unit
28. 8.56		112 Squadron, Bruggen
29. 5.57		Flight Commander, 20 Squadron, Oldenburg
20. 3.58		Central Flying School, Little Rissington
1. 7.58	Squadron Leader	
8. 9.58		OC 1 Squadron, 2 Flying Training School, Syerston
21. 3.60		Examiner, Central Flying School
15. 1.62		52 Course, RAF Staff College Bracknell
7. 1.63		PA 3e, Air Secretary's Department
16. 9.63		PA 1, Air Secretary's Department
1. 1.64	Wing Commander	
15.11.65		226 Operational Conversion Unit, Coltishall
23. 5.66		OC 23 Squadron, Leuchars

Promotions		Appointments
1. 7.68	Group Captain	
15. 7.68		OC RAF Gutersloh
11. 1.71		Royal College of Defence Studies
14. 2.72		Air Ministry, (Air Defence Study)
13. 9.72	Air Commodore	Director of Air Staff Plans
11. 8.75	Air Vice-Marshal	Commandant, RAF Staff College, Bracknell
10. 3.77		Assistant Chief of Staff (Plans & Policy), SHAPE
30. 8.78	Air Marshal	AOCinC RAF Support Command
15. 9.80	Air Chief Marshal	AOCinC Strike Command
15.10.82		Chief of the Air Staff
15.10.85	Marshal of the Royal Air Force	Appointment relinquished

Marshal of the Royal Air Force Sir David Craig

GCB, OBE, MA

Date of Birth: 17 September 1929

Service honours and Awards:

Queen's Commendation (12.6.65), OBE (10.6.67), GCB (16.6.84)

Promotions		Appointments
19. 9.51	Pilot Officer	7 Flying Training School, Cottesmore
19. 3.52	Flying Officer	
22. 4.52		203 Advanced Flying School, Driffield
13. 8.52		Central Flying School
19.12.52	Flight Lieutenant	
12. 1.53		209 Advanced Flying School, Weston Zoyland
12. 4.55		226 Operational Conversion Unit
6. 6.55		247 Squadron, Odiham
5. 5.57		2 Guided Weapons Course, Henlow – Manby
14.10.57		North Coates (Guided Weapons duties)
1. 1.59	Squadron Leader	
1. 4.59		Air Defence (Guided Weapons) 2a, Air Ministry
1. 5.61		19 Staff Course, RAF Staff College, Andover
15. 4.62		RAF Flying College, Manby
11. 7.62		231 Operational Conversion Unit, Bassingbourn
10.10.62		230 Operational Conversion Unit, Finningley
28. 1.63		35 Squadron, Coningsby (Flight Commander)
16. 4.63	Wing Commander (Acting)	OC 35 Squadron, Coningsby – Cottesmore
1. 1.64	Wing Commander	
28. 6.65		Military Assistant to Chief of the Defence Staff
1. 1.68	Group Captain	

Promotions		Appointments
8. 3.68		OC RAF College Cranwell
16. 9.70		HQ Far East Command (Operations Plans)
7. 1.72	Air Commodore	OC RAF Akrotiri
8. 1.74		Royal College of Defence Studies
13.12.74	Air Vice-Marshal (Acting)	Ministry of Defence (for staff study)
1. 1.75	Air Vice-Marshal	
22. 3.75		Assistant Chief of Air Staff (Operations), Ministry of Defence
5. 7.78		AOC 1 Group
3. 5.80	Air Marshal (Acting)	Vice Chief of Air Staff
1. 1.81	Air Marshal	
20. 9.82	Air Chief Marshal (Acting)	AOCinC Strike Command
1. 1.83	Air Chief Marshal	
15.10.85		Chief of the Air Staff
14.11.88	Marshal of the Royal Air Force	
9.12.88		Chief of the Defence Staff

Bibliography

The War in the Air, by Raleigh and Jones – Oxford 1922-1937

Trenchard, Man of Vision, by Andrew Boyle – Collins 1962

From Many Angles, the Autobiography of Sir Frederick Sykes – Harrap 1942

British Air Policy between the Wars, by H Montgomery Hyde – Heinemann 1976

Swifter than Eagles, a biography of Sir John Salmond, by John Laffin – Blackwood 1964

The Royal Air Force 1939-45, Vols 1-3, by Denis Richards and Hilary Saunders – HMSO, 1953/1974

The Right of the Line, by John Terraine – Hodder & Stoughton 1985

The Royal Air Force and Two World Wars, by Sir Maurice Dean – Cassell 1979

Dowding, Leader of the Few, by Basil Collier 1957

Dowding and the Battle of Britain, by Robert Wright 1969

Portal of Hungerford, by Denis Richards – Heinemann 1977

Bomber Offensive, by MRAF Sir Arthur Harris – Collins 1947

Bomber Harris, by Dudley Saward – Buchan & Enright, 1984

Years of Combat, the Autobiography of Sholto Douglas, Vol I – Collins 1963

Years of Command, the Autobiography of Sholto Douglas Vol II – Collins 1966

Tedder, by Roderic Owen – Collins 1952

With Prejudice, the War Memoirs of Lord Tedder – Cassell – 1966

Air Power and Armies, by Wg Cdr J C Slessor – OUP 1936

Strategy for the West, by MRAF Sir John Slessor – Cassell 1954

The Central Blue, by MRAF Sir John Slessor – Cassell 1956

The Great Deterrent, by MRAF Sir John Slessor – Cassell 1957

My Life, by MRAF Sir Dermot Boyle – privately published 1989

In the Midst of Things, by Lord Cameron – Hodder & Stoughton 1986

Flight from the Middle East, by Sir David Lee – HMSO 1980

Eastward, by Sir David Lee – HMSO 1984

Wings in the Sun, by Sir David Lee – HMSO 1989

Index

Duxford: 66, 75
East Kirkby: 85
Eastchurch: 36
Eastleigh: 76
Fayid: 66
Fassberg: 90
Felixstowe: 70
Finningley: 83
Grangemouth: 75, 76
Graveley: 85
Gutersloh: 88, 91
Halton (Apprentice School): 23, 15,
   16, 29, 90
Hawarden: 75
Hawkinge: 47, 51
Hendon: 9, 19, 41
High Wycombe: 78, 92, 93, 98
Hillingdon (11 Gp): 57
Hendon: 3, 8, 9, 19, 31, 40, 41, 46,
   51, 55, 65
Henlow (Technical College): 56, 72,
   82, 95
Hinaidi: 51
Hornchurch: 65
Invergordon: 70
Ismailia: 48
Jever: 90
Kenley: 19, 31, 75
Khormaksar: 77, 87
Leconfield: 66, 80
Leuchars: 91
Linton-on-Ouse: 72
Little Rissington: 91
Lough Erne: 70
Manby: 77, 78, 95
Manston: 31
Marham: 61: 86
Martlesham Heath: 80
Mersa Matruh: 81
Mildenhall: 65
Milfield: 76
Montrose: 80
Mount Pleasant: 93
Mosul: 9, 51
Netheravon: 41, 70
Nicosia: 76
North Coates: 96
North Weald: 31, 56, 62, 66
Northolt: 41, 65
Northwood: 93
Oban: 70
Odiham: 53, 62, 95
Old Sarum: 81
Pembroke Dock: 27, 70
Preston: 47
Ranchi (Bengal): 76
Redhill: 80
Rudloe Manor: 47
Scampton: 52

Scone: 80
Sealand: 65
Shallufa: 76
Skellingthorpe: 85
St Eval: 71
Stanley: 88, 93
Stornaway: 71
Stradishall: 52
Sullom Voe: 70
Suttons Farm: 41
Syerston: 91
Tafaroui: 71
Tangmere: 56, 62
Ternhill: 56
Thornaby: 65
Turnhouse: 52
Upavon: 1, 8, 12, 15, 41, 82
Uxbridge: 9, 19, 60
Waddington: 61, 94, 96
Warmwell: 76
Watton: 60
West Raynham: 95
Weston Zoyland: 95
White Waltham: 91
Wittering: 56, 75, 80
Worthy Down: 27
Establishments/Units:
   No 1 Mobile Operations Room: 56
   No 1 Officers' Advanced Training
      School: 56
   No 9 Bombing & Gunnery School:
      75
   No 13 Operational Training Unit: 60
   No 52 Operational Training Unit: 66
   No 73 (Fighter) Operational
      Training Unit: 66
   No 1657 Heavy Conversion Unit: 52
   Air Armament School: 36
   Central Bombing Establishment: 61
   Central Fighter Establishment: 67
   Central Gunnery School: 65
   Central Photographic
      Establishment: 76
   Hudson Operational Training Units:
      71
   Metropolitan Sector: 62
   Operational Evaluation Unit
      (Boscombe Down): 98
   Photographic Reconnaissance Unit:
      33
   Spitfire Operational Training Unit:
      75
   Tornado Training Establishment
      (TTE) (Cottesmore): 97
RAF Regiment: 88,91
Royal Flying Corps (RFC), xi, xiv, 1, 2, 5,
   6, 7, 8, 11, 12, 15, 19, 23, 27, 31, 36, 41,
   44